# Promise
## That

# YOU
## WILL
# SING

# ABOUT

ALSO BY MILES MARSHALL LEWIS

*Scars of the Soul Are Why Kids Wear Bandages When They Don't Have Bruises*

*There's a Riot Goin' On*

# Promise That You Will Sing About Me.

## The Power and Poetry of Kendrick Lamar

## Miles Marshall Lewis

ST. MARTIN'S PRESS
NEW YORK

*For Kalel and Lucas*

First published in the United States by St. Martin's Press, an imprint of St. Martin's Publishing Group

PROMISE THAT YOU WILL SING ABOUT ME. Copyright © 2021 by Miles Marshall Lewis. All rights reserved. Printed in China. For information, address St. Martin's Publishing Group, 120 Broadway, New York, NY 10271.

www.stmartins.com

Photographs from Unsplash. Unsplash grants you an irrevocable, nonexclusive, worldwide copyright license to download, copy, modify, distribute, perform, and use photos from Unsplash for free, including for commercial purposes, without permission from or attributing the photographer or Unsplash. Illustrations by Andrés Vera Martínez and Jibola Fagbamiye

The Library of Congress Cataloging-in-Publication Data is available upon request.

ISBN 978-1-250-23168-0 (hardcover)
ISBN 978-1-250-23169-7 (ebook)

Our books may be purchased in bulk for promotional, educational, or business use. Please contact your local bookseller or the Macmillan Corporate and Premium Sales Department at 1-800-221-7945, extension 5442, or by email at MacmillanSpecialMarkets@macmillan.com.

First Edition: 2021

10 9 8 7 6 5 4 3 2 1

# Table of Contents

# Miles Marshall Lewis

# Introduction

Kendrick Lamar sits back in a black leather armchair reading up on the quest for a black Christ. The twists of his kinky Afro freshly twisted, lounging comfortably in a gray athleisure suit, he flips through pages older than his twenty-seven years: a vintage 1969 *Ebony* magazine. Typical L.A. sunshine beams outside Milk Studios near Santa Monica Boulevard as the same publication photographs Kendrick for a summer 2015 cover. Someone on his Top Dawg Entertainment team replaces a carefully curated playlist of Miles Davis, Duke Ellington, and Parliament-Funkadelic with the latest Young Thug mixtape so he can loosen up, and it works. Kendrick stands to his full five-and-a-half feet and starts waving his arms animatedly for the clicking photographer as if onstage.

*Ebony*'s editor-in-chief asked me to create that rejected playlist well beforehand, suggesting songs made up from the influences on Kendrick's latest record, *To Pimp a Butterfly*. Media outlets had already reported specific jazz and funk inspirations behind the album—Miles, P-Funk, Sly Stone, John Coltrane—but clearly he'd already moved on. At Milk I'd wanted to be a witness, a fly on the wall, knowing we wouldn't speak until much later at a Santa Monica recording studio. By the end of the photo shoot, Kendrick felt so comfortable in the Robert Geller suit chosen by the fashion director that he wore it to our meet-up at UMG Iovine Studio and into the night, never to return it.

My crash course in Kendrick Lamar Duckworth involved streaming a crucial MTV interview, a critical relistening of his first major label album *good kid, m.A.A.d city*, and looping the six-week-old *To Pimp a Butterfly* on iPhone repeat. Hit singles like "Swimming Pools (Drank)," "Poetic Justice," and "Bitch, Don't Kill My Vibe" dominated radio for years, I knew them well. Black Lives Matter rallies across the country had not yet adopted "Alright" as an anthem, but it was my personal favorite from the new album. I never delved into his earliest mixtapes from the early aughts or his independent debut album, *Section.80*. My deadline was too tight, our interview meant to focus squarely on *To Pimp a Butterfly*.

That night I asked him, *You've been compared to Nas, and he once recorded "The Unauthorized Biography of Rakim." If you recorded another MC's unauthorized biography, whose would it be?*, not knowing he'd already done "Kurupted," an ode to the 1990s Death Row Records rapper Kurupt, four years earlier. The faux pas—not knowing my interview subject down to the smallest minutiae—was forgiven. For a millennial like Kendrick, *Ebony* was probably that staple of every black grandparent's living room table, right beside the *Jet* magazine and the bowl of peppermints. Before *good kid, m.A.A.d city* in 2012, he'd already been known all over the rap blogosphere and among hard-core hiphop fans for mixtapes like *C4*, *Training Day*, and *Overly Dedicated*. But he wouldn't have expected his grandparents' pop culture bible to be as informed as, say, DJBooth. We touched on more universal areas instead. I asked him at one point about opening himself up as an African-American male.

*Who do you feel truly comfortable talking to? As men, generally we speak to each other about sports, sex, music, movies, maybe politics, and that's it*, I said.

Sitting behind an enormous mixing board full of equalizer knobs and levels, he leaned back thoughtfully. "I can't even answer that," he admitted. "With all the good things my father has taught me, this is one of the things he taught me that he shouldn't have: that I can't really confide to him in an emotional way, you know? My brothers and I were taught not to really show those types of feelings as men, especially toward another man, because then you're vulnerable. It's crazy. Most men will go to a woman." Three months back, Kendrick had just become engaged to Whitney Alford, his Centennial High School sweetheart. "It's really about trust issues too," he continued. "I still need to figure that out."

Top Dawg Entertainment general manager Roberto Reyes—known within the camp as retOne—transported me from the Hollywood photography studio to the

Santa Monica recording studio, caravanning close behind Kendrick. The Uber gods were responsible for my trip back to the Montrose Hotel in West Hollywood. Right before thumbing in my coordinates on the rideshare app, we hit a groove about South Africa. In early February 2014 he'd visited Johannesburg, Cape Town, and Durban for a trio of concerts, his first time on the continent. The trip influenced some of the rhythms and thematic breadth of *To Pimp a Butterfly* (as well as the Grammy-nominated soundtrack he'd later curate for *Black Panther*, the top-grossing film of 2018). The album closer, "Mortal Man," referenced his visit to Robben Island and what he'd seen in the prison cell of the late Nelson Mandela.

"It was just an overwhelming feeling to me, like we were really home," he told me. "That's why I called one of the tracks on the new album 'Momma,' which symbolizes the Motherland. When we watch certain commercials, we're shown the bad parts of Africa. That makes people born in the States feel like they shouldn't go there. Africa does have poverty-stricken areas and I've seen that. But at the same time, we were never told that it's also one of the most beautiful places on Earth—the land and the people.

**Some of the children I saw on my trip didn't have much, but they were so happy. They were playing like they were going to live forever.**

I thought about how much we stress about in America, while those kids are enjoying life with no material possessions."

Making parallels with my upbringing in the urban-blighted Bronx during the 1970s and '80s with Kendrick's native Compton in the 1980s and '90s, I explained how living abroad expanded my sense of self. My personal journey took me to France, relocating to Paris for seven years. Asking *Where would you go?*, his response was immediate. "Where would I settle? If I left the States, I would go to Cape Town. Seriously."

*To Pimp a Butterfly* marked a genuinely artistic left turn, a creative gamble the young MC won hands down. With 2012's more mainstream, Grammy Award–winning *good kid, m.A.A.d city* (number one on *Billboard*'s album chart) and its catchy singles, no one expected a follow-up like *To Pimp a Butterfly*. The album's "u" dug deeper lyrically than anywhere near necessary to maintain his position as the torchbearer of West Coast hiphop, spewing self-critical barbs straight from his id that revealed bouts of depression and poetic self-doubt. "For Free? (Interlude)," produced by noted saxophonist Terrace Martin, featured bebop improvisation that sounded like an outtake from jazz legend Max Roach's 1971 album *We Insist!* (Martin had his hands in five songs on Kendrick's sixteen-track album, joined by young lions like Thundercat, Kamasi Washington, Robert Glasper, and Flying Lotus.) I already knew that, growing up, his parents had mainly exposed him to the soul of Marvin Gaye and the Isley Brothers, the street reportage of Tupac Shakur and N.W.A. Where'd the jazz come from?

"One of the producers was telling me I was already a jazz musician based on my cadence and how I put songs together," he answered. "I was doing it without even knowing the history of jazz or studying those artists for years." When I asked him about being an old soul at twenty-seven, he agreed. "I think it's just the blood of my ancestors. I've always been drawn to older people. I was always at the house parties, always in the older crowds, always around my uncles and my parents. I even carried myself a little differently around the kids I played with. When I was probably nine years old, I played football with kids that were around sixteen." He was also the rare tweener on his block watching Asian action movies from the 1970s like *Master of the Flying Guillotine* and *Five Deadly Venoms*, and the era's raunchy blaxploitation films by comedian Dolemite.

A moratorium on discussing Kendrick Lamar's verse on the Big Sean single "Control" was baked into the interview ground rules handed down from Top Dawg Entertainment president Dave Free even before I'd flown in from New York City. By then he was tired of talking about his instantly infamous three-minute harangue from 2013, targeting eleven different rappers, including Big Sean himself. ("I'm usually homeboys with the same niggas I'm rhymin' with/But this is hiphop, and them niggas should know what time it is/And that goes for Jermaine Cole, Big K.R.I.T., Wale/Pusha-T, Meek Millz, A$AP Rocky, Drake/Big Sean, Jay Electron', Tyler, Mac Miller/I got love for you all, but I'm tryna murder you niggas/Tryna make sure your core fans never heard of you niggas/They don't wanna hear not one more noun or verb from you niggas.") The verse—on a song that wasn't even Kendrick's to begin with—sparked over a dozen responses, giving 2010s hiphop its first major upheaval moment.

As we sat together in the studio, most conversations about Kendrick outside those soundproof walls still centered on the aftershock of "Control" and the avant-garde direction of *To Pimp a Butterfly*. When awards season arrived months later, the Grammys honored Kendrick with eleven nominations (more than any rapper in a single year ever), including (as with *good kid, m.A.A.d city*) his second nod for Album of the Year. By December, President Barack Obama would single out the album's "How Much a Dollar Cost" as his favorite song of 2015 in *People* magazine. At sixteen years old, Kendrick offered his 2003 mixtape *Y.H.N.I.C. (Hub City Threat: Minor of the Year)* onto the internet. But he'd only become widely known to the pop mainstream in the three years since the release of *good kid, m.A.A.d city*, and already his fame and respect level from Compton to the Grammy Awards to the White House accorded him the anointed status of a Jay-Z. In another three years, at thirty, Kendrick Lamar would accept the Pulitzer Prize for Music for *DAMN.* (his proper follow-up to *To Pimp a Butterfly*)—the first non-classical or jazz artist ever to win.

But all that came later. Kendrick met me in the studio that night because he had work to do; he's the type of artist who's always in the studio with work to do. Far from itching to get to it, Kendrick gave me his full attention, a master of remaining in the moment. So I asked him about that.

**Do you meditate? How do you quiet the noise around you?**

"Yeah," he admitted. "It's as simple as turning everything off, sitting in a room by yourself, and actually thinking about your accomplishments. In this business and this lifestyle, it's so fast that you actually forget you're in it. You're always thinking of the next move, the next play, the next song, the next lyric, the next radio station—"

**You're never in the moment.**

"You're never in the moment, and that's a lot when you're losing out on being grateful for it. So sometimes you have to literally sit in a room—I'm sure a lot of artists do this—and really just meditate on yourself and your connection with the higher power and where you want to go."

**Where do you get your spiritual foundation?**

"I was baptized a few years ago," he said. "I got saved in a parking lot, like I said on *good kid, m.A.A.d city*. The more I started going through my own things in life, my faith got put to the test, and I had to believe that God—my lord and savior, Jesus Christ—is real in my heart, and I can't run from that. I'll always put that in my music or it just wouldn't be right. People can take it or leave it, I really don't care. Because it's for me to put it on records. And I will continue to put more of a spiritual nature in my music."

Soon my car arrived and, after an obligatory social media selfie, we parted ways. But little tidbits kept revealing themselves as my driver waited.

Kendrick had recently met with Prince in Minneapolis at Paisley Park Studios. The legendary rock star had committed to appearing on *To Pimp a Butterfly*'s "Complexion (A Zulu Love)," but the two spent so much time conversing that they lost their time window. Their more recent meeting was too private for Kendrick to share any details about. Four months later I'd interview Prince at his famous home studio complex, and he was equally reserved about the time spent with his fellow Gemini. ("Kendrick, this is his year now," Prince told me. "I asked him to come up here just to visit. I told him, 'You got the whole year. Don't worry about it. Ain't nobody gonna bother you.' We talked about a lot of stuff.") On September 30, 2014, Prince and his 3rdEyeGirl band played an album release concert on a Yahoo live stream for one of his final albums; Kendrick Lamar rhymed guest verses alongside him performing "What's My Name." Initially Prince held disdain for rap music, and his hiphop collaborators were a precious few: Common, Chuck D, Eve, Q-Tip, Doug E. Fresh, and Kendrick Lamar among them.

Prince would only be alive for another twelve months, but naturally we couldn't have known. Instead, we walked outside discussing the death of Michael Jackson.

"It was a trip, man. I was still in Compton at the time, going back and forth to the studio," he said. "I remember going into the house and it was on the news. But it didn't really hit me until I saw a grown man close to shedding a tear, if not shedding a tear. And that was my father."

That night, transcribing our interview in a hotel room near Sunset Boulevard way past midnight, my gut feeling told me Kendrick was also still toiling away back at the studio with TDE in-house producer Mark "Sounwave" Spears. Maybe he was working on one of the tracks from his next studio album, 2017's *DAMN*. Maybe he was working on his verses for the remix to Taylor Swift's "Bad Blood," or guest bars for songs from

TDE labelmates Ab-Soul, Jay Rock, or ScHoolboy Q.

But he was working.

Tupac Shakur once swaggered his way through the mob outside the Slauson Super Mall, fresh out of jail on over a million dollars bail. A remix of "California Love" blared through the humid air of that infamous Compton swap meet, Shakur readjusting his bowler hat and lip synching. Hometown hero Dr. Dre also mugged for the cameras and word spread quickly: Death Row

Records had a music video happening. Bloods, Crips, school kids, groupies, and grandmas crowded all around the video production. One young dad, a former Gangster Disciple from the South Side of Chicago, lifted his beaming eight-year-old son onto his shoulders and pointed to the rap stars in their gleaming black Bentley. The hyperactive scene opened the floodgates of the kid's imagination, and for him, nothing was ever the same again.

That kid, of course, was little Kendrick Duckworth circa November 1995.

Born June 17, 1987, Kendrick Lamar stands as the millennial generation's continuation of 1990s hiphop luminaries like Tupac Shakur, Jay-Z, Biggie Smalls, Nas, and Eminem, all of whom he cites as influences. With the genre currently splintered to a large degree into trap and mumble rap styles, emphasis on high-level lyricism is at a premium. But Lamar consistently raises the bar, couching his rhymes in eclectic backdrops of jazz- and funk-influenced rhythms and a series of creatively complex concept albums. There's no mistaking that Lamar stands at the vanguard of modern-day hiphop alongside any other maverick or populist rapper one cares to name (past collaborators Kanye West, Drake, and J. Cole included). Full of biographical narrative and cultural analysis, *Promise That You Will Sing About Me* tracks the gradual rise of the Grammy-winning MC, directly analyzing his racialized musical life and the evolving ideas about hiphop and race that made his Pulitzer win possible.

A literal child of the riotous aftermath of the Rodney King verdict and Louis Farrakhan's Million Man March, the legion of Kendrick's influences also includes September 11, 2001 and the Osama bin Laden manhunt, the effects of policies by presidents Bill Clinton and George W. Bush on the inner city, the unlikely rise of Barack Obama as America's first black president, and the unlikelier ascent of the United States' first reality TV president, Donald Trump. Biggie and Tupac, Michael Jackson and Prince left seismic sinkholes in the bedrock of pop culture that Kendrick has done his part to fill. (*Thriller* received twelve Grammy nominations in 1984; *To Pimp a Butterfly*, in 2016, garnered eleven. No mere backpack rapper, he earned $58 million in 2017 according to *Forbes*, second only to Jay-Z and Diddy as the richest MC of the year.) Other touchstones include the formation of Black Lives Matter; the tragic deaths of Trayvon Martin, Sandra Bland, Eric Garner, Oscar Grant, and scores more victimized African Americans; the proliferation of social media; and even

**19**

the Afrofuturistic new black pride sparked by *Black Panther*, whose Album of the Year Grammy-nominated soundtrack Lamar produced. These formative events of his lifetime are representative of what's shaped his generation as a whole. Kendrick captures the zeitgeist of our time by blending all these stimuli together in a multitudinous mash-up.

*Promise That You Will Sing About Me* works its way through all these details, with a sharp focus on the larger cultural narrative at work. Part biography, part critical examination, this book uses his personal story and artistic legacy to make universal observations about this moment of racial history from one of the most insightful artists of our time.

"The times that we are in, it's something that you can only feel in the air," Kendrick said to me in parting, talking about the responsibility on his shoulders felt in the past by Bob Dylan, Kurt Cobain, and other generational voices. "You don't even have to talk about it. You don't need the news or the internet to watch it. You can walk outside and just feel it. These are the same times that I believe Marvin Gaye and them felt, just in a whole other generational perspective. And to carry on that type of legacy is only right. I am from Compton. I am from the inner city, the ghetto. And if I can use my platform to carry on a legacy and talk about something that's real, I have to do that, period."

Miles Marshall Lewis
Harlem, New York
August 2021

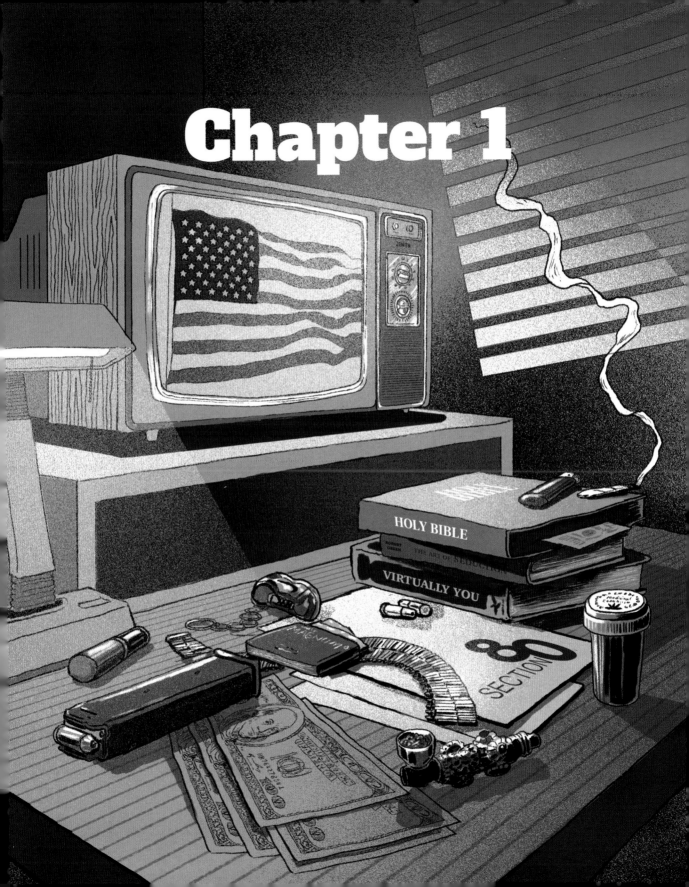

# Ronald Reagan Era

**W**ay back in the Ronald Reagan era, somewhere in the Deep South, there once was a crowded college campus filled with freshman from all over young black America. On a slight hill rising above Martin Luther King, Jr. Drive, small patches of land announced allegiances to African-American fraternities and sororities: an A-shaped concrete plot in the grass for Alpha Phi Alpha; a huge redbrick horseshoe for Omega Psi Phi; Greek letters spray-painted pink and green down the side of an oak tree for Alpha Kappa Alpha, and so on. Students file out of a stately administration building sporting purple beanies—a freshman first-week tradition at this school—pinned to their high-top fades, asymmetrical perms and mushroom bobs. One couple breaks from the crowd, strolling down the hill's winding pathway to a parking lot.

The skinny seventeen-year-old boy, fresh out of high school, flirts with the freckle-faced woman five years his senior. Teenage acne scars his cheeks like razor burn; he's too young to realize he's not getting anywhere. In the confines of her red Nissan Sentra, the scent of the woman's curl activator overpowers her perfume. She pops a new cassette tape into her car stereo: *Eazy-Duz-It*, the debut album by Compton's own Eazy-E. The boy has only heard "Boyz-n-the-Hood," that album's first single, banging in the dorm rooms of kids from California, and his elitist New York City ears are unimpressed with the Jheri-curled MC's nihilist, cartoonish lyrics and whiny tone. His odds with the woman sink even lower; she smiles his ignorance away and turns the music up louder.

The year is 1988, at Morris Brown College in Atlanta. The rap snob with the bad skin is me; the sister with the educational body hails from Vallejo, California—hence the hometown pride. Little Kendrick Lamar Duckworth is a year old, and the soup of Californian hiphop he later swims in is just starting to simmer. His mother, Paula Oliver, might be in Compton breastfeeding him that day to *Eazy-Duz-It* or *Straight Outta Compton*, the weeks-old debut of local bad boys N.W.A. His father, Kenneth Duckworth, could already be working at the Kentucky Fried Chicken his firstborn memorializes three decades later on "DUCKWORTH."

My mansplaining the superiority of Public Enemy, Rakim, and Big Daddy Kane over Eazy-E and his ilk falls on deaf ears in the Nissan, as well it should have. The dormitory where I first heard West Coast rappers like Too Short and Ice-T wouldn't be demolished until 2017. (Morris Brown College lost its accreditation in 2002.) On the ninth floor of the all-male Borders Tower, those MCs' *Born to Mack* and *Rhyme Pays* tapes kept me awake way past midnight, pumping from behind closed doors oozing whiffs of marijuana from underneath. Cultural warfare between students who were aligned with the frenzied production and hyperactive rhyme flows of New York rappers and the laid-back, hardcore aesthetic of California's hiphop artists was real. We were all in the thick of a socially conscious era of MCs from the five boroughs proselytizing for Malcolm X and the Five-Percent Nation over sampled beats by James Brown. Hiphop had been building to that point since 1979's "Rapper's Delight" and, for all any of us knew, might stay that way forever, the final step in its development. Outliers ruled too—the gangster tale "P.S.K. What Does It Mean?" by Philadelphia's Schoolly D, for example—but they were rare. I'd grown up in the Bronx, hiphop's celebrated origin point, never considering that the genre birthed by my neighborhood would ever be truly mastered by anyone outside the tri-state area. When I left New York City behind for Atlanta in the summer of '88,

Public Enemy's newly released *It Takes a Nation of Millions to Hold Us Back* was rap's holy grail (considered the greatest hiphop album of all time for years to come). It took students from all over the country cohabitating in the dorm, and college DJs intent on pleasing horny, sweaty, teenage party people from a nationwide pool, to turn me onto E-40, 2 Live Crew, Eazy-E, Ice-T, Too Short, N.W.A, J. J. Fad, and Sir Mix-a-Lot—most of whom hailed from sunny California.

Decades later, Hollywood crowned N.W.A with the 2015 biopic *Straight Outta Compton*; there is no Public Enemy movie. According to *Forbes*, Dr. Dre—responsible for their classic debut album and so much more—is currently worth $800 million. His last great contribution to hiphop culture: signing underground rapper Kendrick Lamar in 2012 and releasing his first major label album, *good kid, m.A.A.d city*, on his Aftermath Entertainment label.

I matured with hiphop in the 1980s and '90s; I remember tides turning clearly. Cultural ambassador Fab Five Freddy (graffiti artist, one-time MC, Jean-Michel Basquiat buddy) beamed into living rooms around the country hosting *Yo! MTV Raps* and introducing scores of golden-age rappers to all the teenage rebels, geeks, goths, and trust-fund babies of the suburbs. MTV's show was the great equalizer, according equal respect to Geto Boys (from Houston), Tone Lōc (Los Angeles), Will Smith (Philly), Digital Underground (Oakland), De La Soul (Long Island) and any other comers. Ice Cube, the most talented pen in N.W.A, enlisted Public Enemy's New York–based production team in 1990 for his first solo masterpiece, *AmeriKKKa's Most Wanted*—early evidence that rap fans weren't being asked to pick sides. That didn't stop some of us from doing so anyway. But the year I turned up my nose at the first

Dr. Dre production I ever heard in a cute Cali freshman's hooptie, hiphop slowly snaked its way out of the bottle of my hometown, granting champagne wishes and caviar dreams to aspiring MCs rubbing on microphones all across America.

Hardheaded hiphop lovers still stayed territorial to the bitter end, otherwise known as *The Chronic*. On a seven-hour road trip down to Mardi Gras, a posse of frat boys crammed into a clown car speeding down I-59 playing Dr. Dre's magnum opus on repeat. I resisted. I argued (a losing argument) funk godfather George Clinton's source material as the only good thing about the album besides Snoop Dogg. By Tennessee I was a convert. Hiphop's politically conscious era was dead. There's a conspiracy theory as to why, subscribed to by the same types who believe in the antebellum speech of slaveholder Willie Lynch[1] : white supremacists in power at record labels made a deliberate decision to sideline empowering rap music, promoting and investing in content that celebrated gangster anarchy, female subjugation, and black-on-black death instead. *The Chronic* promoted all that, sure, but with Dr. Dre and co.'s Dolemite-like sense of humor.

---

[1] "Discipline the disobedient, hang 'em like Willie Lynch"—"Play With Fire."

While Public Enemy's production team disassembled and cultural-nationalist groups like Poor Righteous Teachers floundered, California rose higher and higher. Hollywood did as much as Compton to speed along the process. The Academy Awards made the late John Singleton the youngest director in history to be nominated as best director for *Boyz n the Hood*, a tragedy about the hard life in South Central Los Angeles, starring Ice Cube. *Juice* made a movie star out of Tupac Shakur, the handsome, charismatic MC behind the previous year's standout album *2Pacalypse Now*. A wave of so-called hood films washed over Tinseltown, glorifying gang life and ghetto living while humanizing those situations at the same time. Cali hiphop was literally the soundtrack: new voices like Cypress Hill, MC Eiht, and DJ Quik. *The Chronic* was cinematic in scope in and of itself, remixing the foundation of funk music with wormy synthesizer lines à la P-Funk keyboardist Bernie Worrell, with a thunderous bottom and addictive hooks. Picture Kendrick Duckworth, age five or six, doing awkward little kid dances at his parents' house parties in L.A. way past his bedtime. From Compton to Brooklyn—with "Nuthin' but a 'G' Thang," "Let Me Ride," "Fuck wit Dre Day" and the rest—*The Chronic* was the party record of 1993.

Of the sociopolitical events from the 1990s that were inescapable, my memories always marry the political to the personal. The day I decided to go in search of some faraway tattoo parlor on the outskirts of Atlanta, trudging over train tracks in the heat on a side of town I'd never seen, the city was literally on fire. The date was April 29, 1992, and I never got that tattoo. (The parlor closed early.) By the time I arrived at the address, it was clear to me something felt off. Stone Mountain was rumored to be Ku Klux Klan territory, but I wasn't anywhere near there. Yet I had the distinct impression that white eyes were staring. I felt fear. Theirs.

"This isn't the way to solve your problems," a middle-aged white lady told me through a cracked car window. Not in anger; more like pleading. The traffic light changed and she sped off. (The only other time strangers in Atlanta had ever spoken to me from the safety of a speeding car, they shouted "nigger.")

Tattooless, I rode MARTA public transit back to my off-campus apartment on Buford Highway. My roommates already sat transfixed by the TV, and finally I understood. All four police officers accused of assault and excessive force against California motorist Rodney King just got acquitted. Our local Korean-owned liquor store, smack dab in the middle of the Atlanta University Center, burned down to the ground after students and folks in the surrounding housing projects liberated the place of all its high-end libations. A close friend launched his pro photography career that day, shooting uprisings all over town and selling his prints to the *Atlanta Journal-Constitution*. The final episode of *The Cosby Show* aired that night. It was almost the last thing on anybody's mind. By the midnight hour, late-night news pundits were poring over Ice Cube lyrics for answers. By May 4 police arrested over twelve thousand people, with more than two thousand injured and sixty-three dead. Nationwide, the uprising resulted in over one billion dollars' worth of damage, with more than thirty-seven hundred buildings damaged or destroyed by fire.

The hindsight of time was never necessary to infer that the O. J. Simpson verdict three years later served as a community payback for the morally corrupt Rodney King decision. We'd all seen the two-minute tape of officers attacking King with nightsticks over and over and beating him down to the ground. The cops' acquittal only polarized us into those who expected justice and others who assumed from the start that the court system would be as corrupt as the Los Angeles Police Department. The script of the O. J. Simpson case started with similar story beats, only in real time.

On June 17, 1994, I remember sitting in a northeast Bronx living room with a pro bono lawyer, running through the sexual assault of my girlfriend's teenage sister. There was a TV on mute, a program interrupted, then a surreal high-speed chase down an L.A. freeway. We expected a car crash, shots fired at tires, a suicide. Arrested for killing his ex-wife and a friend, O. J. Simpson hired a high-profile attorney, and the televised trial turned into the must-see TV event of the year. Hiphop had always been my Greek chorus, the soundtrack running in the background of life. The music started overtaking pop culture in the 1990s, in my twenties. So my mind conflates the Simpson chase with the shooting of Tupac Shakur later that November. The murder trial started in January 1995 and ended in October, the month Tupac got out on bail from a sexual abuse sentence. When the O. J. verdict came down, I was a study-abroad law student in London, still disappointed that I'd miss the Million Man March in two weeks.

*"Kendrick's environment isn't safe. It might be a little gentrified right now, but it wasn't safe. And he had the wherewithal to observe as opposed to participate, whereas his contemporaries participated. That perspective kinda elevated gangster rap in a way for him because you can relate to that. He knows cats who have bodies on their guns and has seen friends who have been killed by certain things. As the observer, he has a special place in being able to talk gangster shit and not be a participant."*
—KEVIN L. CLARK

*"Kendrick has amassed an audience that's as varied as it is massive, and he means something different to everyone simply because everyone is listening. That is his power. Where the themes in his music or the presentation of his persona are concerned, some see through the performance, while others see his sincerity. Herein lies the buffer between Kendrick and ridicule—whether his lyrics as they pertain to religion, spirituality, or any of his personal ideologies take form as ignorance, intellect, or inspiration, it's marked by authenticity. People look for 'the real,' no matter how it looks."*
—IVIE ANI

Alongside episodes of *Martin* and *The Simpsons*, these were the TV news reports echoing through Kendrick Duckworth's house the years he fell in love with rapping. He may have paid no attention to President Bill Clinton's 1994 crime bill incarcerating black and brown offenders at unprecedented rates—he was seven, after all—but his Compton community certainly felt its effects. At the very least Monica Lewinsky registered on his radar come 1998.[2] However he internalized the Rodney King riots[3], O. J. going free[4], the release of Nelson Mandela, the black film renaissance, the HIV announcements of Magic Johnson and Eazy-E, or any other topical touchstones of the 1990s, young Kendrick definitely took note of Tupac. When Death Row Records shut down the Slauson swap meet in November '95 to film a video for the "California Love" remix, twenty minutes away from Lamar's powder blue three-bedroom house at 1612 West 137th Street, it was no mistake his father rushed him right over in his Cadillac Seville.

Paula Oliver and Kenneth Duckworth, high school sweethearts from Chicago, married on November 4, 1991. By then they'd already moved out west to California, with five hundred dollars between them, sometime in 1984, on an

---

[2] "Manipulated Bill Clinton with desires"—"King Kunta."
[3] "Ever since the Rodney King riots/Mind militant, nigga don't try it"—"Intro (HOVA Song Freestyle)." Also see "Couple stolen TVs and a seat belt for my safety/Played the passenger, I think it's five years after '87/Do the math, '92, don't you be lazy"—"County Building Blues."
[4] "A baller slash killer like O. J. Simpson/Close to the mic like Scottie Pippen"—"Go DJ."

Amtrak to San Bernardino with two extra-large garbage bags for suitcases. Duckworth grew up in Chicago's infamous Robert Taylor Homes, and was reportedly a member of Chi-Town's Gangster Disciples gang. He left all that behind for the Golden State, where he and Oliver struggled to make ends meet.

They scrapped their plan for San Bernardino when Paula's sister Tina (who lived an hour away in Compton) offered to put them up in a local hotel until they found their footing. For years Paula and Kenny surfed McJobs (some legal—KFC, McDonald's—others not so much) sleeping in motels or their own car or public parks. The young couple eventually availed themselves to Section 8 public housing and the city's welfare rolls, but they worked. Come June 17, 1987, their first son, Kendrick Lamar Duckworth, was born at Dominguez Medical Center in Compton. They named the baby in honor of Edward James Kendrick—better known as Eddie Kendricks, cofounder and lead singer of Motown's legendary vocalists, The Temptations. The ride home introduced baby Kendrick to hiphop, the car stereo blaring '87-era Big Daddy Kane.

*"The new music cartel actually saved the music industry. Eskay, Lowkey, On-Smash, 2DopeBoyz, they made it so that you were excited about music. These guys were providing it in an exclusive way that you weren't gonna find on the radio, the record labels had no access to, and it was all through the comments section of trading and talking about who had what. Twitter was still early in its infancy, so you really couldn't rely on your timeline to tell you what's coming out and when it's coming out. For Kendrick, it was 2DopeBoyz. When TDE were able to put out those first few videos, where Aplusfilmz was on the street directing them, they had the platforms where you were going to see them almost in real time."*
—KEVIN L. CLARK

**31**

Born and raised in westside Compton, young Kendrick Lamar racked up top grades at Ronald E. McNair Elementary School, Vanguard Learning Center and, later, Centennial High. He saw his first murder at five: a man selling drugs near his apartment unit blasted in the chest by a shotgun. He saw his second murder at eight: another young black man ordering fast food at Tam's Burgers, killed while waiting at the drive-thru window. Kendrick has spoken on other incidents. At 15 he got jumped and beat down by a crew at the Avalon swap meet in front of his mother.

She once discovered him in the fetal position crying in the front yard after returning home from being shot at. The Duckworths evicted their own son for two days after police accused him of being involved in a local incident. Those same months recording his first mixtape, Kendrick experienced two house raids by the L.A.P.D., their boots on his back, their beams in his face[5]. For those who live there, sports and music often seem like the only ways to escape the violence of low-income American inner cities. Compton native Arron Afflalo signed with the Detroit Pistons in 2007. Venus and Serena Williams mastered their skills on public tennis courts in their Compton hood. André Young and David Blake graduated Centennial High School in 1983 and '88 respectively; their worldwide fame as Dr. Dre and DJ Quik came later. Two years after cheering Dre and Tupac at the Slauson Super Mall at eight years old, Kendrick chose music, writing out rhymes in marble composition notebooks and thick sheaves of loose-leaf paper.

A seventh-grade English teacher, Regis Inge, assigned poetry homework Kendrick dashed off in ten minutes. In a sea of his classmates' C's and D's, he received an A, a watershed moment that boosted his confidence with wordplay. He credits the 1998 debut of Yonkers, New York, rapper DMX—*It's Dark and Hell Is Hot*—as the first album to inspire him to

---

[5] "Uncle Bobby got the house raided back in 9-6/Kick in the door/K9s all in the kitchen way before I even heard of Mike Vick."—"Look Out for Detox"

become an MC. Kendrick's trial-and-error journey of styles, inspired primarily by Kurupt, Jay-Z, DMX, Eminem, and Tupac, resulted in his first mixtape at the age of sixteen.

*Y.H.N.I.C. (The Hub City Threat: Minor of the Year)* made for a cumbersome title. In typical mixtape fashion, many of the eleven songs feature the self-proclaimed "young head nigga in charge" rhyming over already familiar rap tracks: Snoop's "Drop It Like It's Hot," Game's "How We Do," Jay-Z's "Hova Song (Intro)," Lloyd Banks's "Work Magic," the Notorious B.I.G.'s "Biggie," and Lil Wayne's "Go DJ." The year 2003 marked the debut of K-Dot and, the year being '03, the internet afforded him a much wider audience than a mixtape would've received even five years earlier.

And Kendrick had help. The local independent label Konkrete Jungle Muzik pressed, marketed, and distributed his mixtape. Dave Free, also enrolled at Centennial High, met Kendrick in the tenth grade through a mutual friend. A DJ with a makeshift home studio and record industry ambitions, Free partnered with K-Dot early to bring his music to Anthony Tiffith, CEO and Top Dawg of Compton indie label Top Dawg Entertainment. Posing as a computer tech, Free disassembled the label head's computer trying to perk his ears with *Hub City Threat* playing on Tiffith's office stereo. Soon a skeptical Top Dawg auditioned K-Dot for two hours, spontaneously emceeing over double-time beats he chose to trip up the young rapper. K-Dot's *Hub City Threat* follow-up, 2005's *Training Day*, became his first TDE mixtape.

The day will come when the mention of Facebook will date this book with a back-in-the-day time stamp. *Hub City Threat* dropped the same year as the launch of Myspace, a social network that needs to be explained at this point, as memory of its onetime internet dominance continues to fade. Myspace, a digital playground not unlike Facebook but much more music friendly, built on the popular advances of previous dotcom social destinations like BlackPlanet and Friendster. As mass media shifted online from the print age at the turn of the century (it seems like just yesterday . . .), the rise of two phenomena turned the possibility of K-Dot spreading his fame beyond the four corners of 137th Street into a stark reality: digital downloads and blogging.

Subscriptions to Spotify, Tidal, Pandora, Apple Music, and the rest are as common now as cable subscription packages. But before the music streaming revolution, an entire evolution leading up to the latest music industry model took place that played to K-Dot's advantage. Napster, the big bang in music file-sharing over the internet, rose in 1999 and came crashing down two short years later. Copyright infringement lawsuits from major record labels brought the site to an end, but the industry learned that they couldn't unring the bell: soon LimeWire (launched in 2000) briefly served the same purpose. In the twenty-first century, songs would (or certainly could) be absolutely free, music piracy made simple courtesy of Megaupload, BitTorrent, and whatever latest method being used as you're reading this page.

## Record labels almost didn't survive this technological insurrection; a handful actually folded.

Along with the rumblings of social networking on Myspace[6], anyone halfway savvy with a broadband connection illegally downloaded any album or single they wanted. Then like-minded music lovers started talking to one another. In 2006 *Time* magazine got cheeky and chose "You" for their annual Person of the Year issue, because the newsmagazine determined that blogging was here to stay. Outside of the personal weblogs that scores of everyday people launched through personal websites and blog-publishing services like Blogger, blogs specially dedicated to music sprouted everywhere. 2DopeBoyz and OnSmash and Nahright refreshed content like they had dedicated newsroom staffs. Pitchfork and Pigeons & Planes became the instantaneous, authoritative voices of music criticism that 1990s tastemakers like *XXL*, *Vibe*, and *The Source* magazines once were. "Blog rap" became a thing, MCs rising to fame on message boards instead of the streets.[7] Music bloggers of the aughts became the first to advocate for Kendrick Lamar in his mixtape period.

*Hub City Threat* didn't quite deserve that advocacy. Plenty of sixteen-year-old rappers from LL Cool J to Earl Sweatshirt proved capable beyond their years on beloved rap projects way back in the beginning of their discographies. K-Dot showed promise, but he wasn't there yet. He mentions Jaguars and Porsches that he couldn't possibly afford and may not have been able to drive. He mentions Nintendo cartridges on "Hovi Baby"—video games would naturally still have been a part of his life. Clichés like "sick like a cancer patient" and "married to rap" appear on the same song ("How We Do"); two different songs mention *A Nightmare on Elm Street*'s Freddy Krueger. Plenty of guns and bitches are mentioned, as well as rap heroes Jay-Z, 50 Cent, Tupac, and the Notorious B.I.G. On "Biggie," K-Dot states he's "been an artist since Prince played in *Color Purple*." For those who haven't seen it, spoiler alert: Prince does not appear in *The Color Purple*. Further, Kendrick wasn't yet born for the release of either *Purple Rain* or *The Color Purple*.

On the contrary, Kendrick was indeed around for *Training Day*, a crime thriller about a crooked narcotics detective in South Central L.A. (both Dr. Dre and Snoop

---

[6] K-Dot's Myspace name was KDOTTDE.

[7] Wale, Kid Cudi, B.o.B and Cali hiphop collective Odd Future also emerged in the blog rap era.

*"You really had to stay tuned to whatever website that you were messing with. 2DopeBoyz were the ones who were already out in the West Coast—Shake being in Las Vegas and Meka being in L.A. They were already hearing about all the people that took a few years to get to New York status. Kendrick's place in all that is being accessible in a way that helped build TDE from the ground up. When they started being able to disseminate this music, you had nowhere else to get it from, making them a priority. You had to rely on them to be able to get you the exclusive. It made the artists that they were covering priceless."*

—KEVIN L. CLARK

Dogg make cameos) that won Denzel Washington his Oscar for best actor. In 2005 the Hub City threat entitled his second mixtape *Training Day*, with snippets of movie dialogue spliced from the DVD. (Denzel's most celebrated line, "King Kong ain't got shit on me," gets quoted toward the end of "Man of the Hour.") Mixtapes aren't strictly for sale; they float around freely on the internet; their non-commercial nature allows them to flout copyright permission laws. On *Training Day*, K-Dot borrows beats liberally from André 3000's "Prototype," Game's "Da Shit," Rakim's classic "Paid in Full," Snoop's "Imagine," Jay-Z's "Get Throwed," Slum Village's "Players," Beastie Boys' "Paul Revere," and Biggie's "Who Shot Ya." The mixtape captures many sophomoric moments. He spits the cringeworthy cliché "if it don't make dollars, then it don't make sense" twice, on "The Best Rapper Alive" and "J. Dilla (Freestyle)." He's back to video games on "Blow Them Horns" ("scared to play Madden on All Pro"). Unbelievably, he brings up *A Nightmare on Elm Street* for the third time on "Imma G." Again the project references luxury Bentleys and Maybachs outside his financial reach, along with tons of drugs, guns, and bitches, plus rap idols galore (Biggie, Tupac, Jay-Z, Dr. Dre, Kanye West, Nas, Dilla).

By happenstance he drops a subliminal clue to a future project, a habit that becomes routine later in his career. In one of the earliest scenes of director Antoine Fuqua's *Training Day*, Denzel's corrupt officer forces a rookie cop (Ethan Hawke, who garnered an Oscar nomination) to smoke angel dust: marijuana laced with the hallucinogen PCP. Kendrick doesn't smoke, partially because of once accidentally puffing on a laced marijuana cigarette. The coincidence may or may not have influenced him naming his second mixtape *Training Day*, but one of two possible meanings of the "m.A.A.d" acronym in his first major label album title stands for "my angel's on angel dust," with lyrics detailing his negative drug experience.

With *Training Day*, K-Dot's talent makes him one of the stronger young MCs of the aughts. He plays with baseball, football, and basketball analogies on "Blood Sport." Named after the French liqueur, "Hpnotiq" starts with a ten-to-one countdown, runs down stories involving hypnosis, then reveals by the end that you, the listener, have spent the past two minutes hypnotized. Instead of rhyming bars like a lyric-generating machine, "Hpnotiq" shows Kendrick's interest in the type of signature conceptual songs he's come to be known for. Name-dropping George Clinton and Kurt Cobain proves K-Dot's radar also detects musicians outside the rap universe. On "Grammy Family (Freestyle)," he even presciently rhymes about signing to Aftermath ("Remember having Aftermath sitting on my porch/But money was barricading my door, I couldn't open it"). Dave Free inserts five interview interludes all throughout *Training Day*, smart promotion for Top Dawg Entertainment as a growing label and K-Dot as one of its marquee artists. TDE president and cofounder Terrence "Punch" Henderson—cousin of TDE's CEO, Anthony "Top Dawg" Tiffith—guests on five tracks ("Dreams," "Blow Them Horns," "Prototype," "Imagine," and "J. Dilla (Freestyle)"); Jay Rock only shows up once ("Imagine"), despite eventually ending up with the wider-spanning rap career.

Speaking of: Two years Kendrick's senior, Jay Rock—born Johnny Reed McKinzie, Jr., in Watts, California—signed to TDE earlier in 2005 after coming to the attention of Top Dawg. When formerly gang-affiliated with the Bounty Hunter Bloods, Jay Rock got locked up on two separate occasions. His career would later become a cautionary tale for Kendrick and a learning curve example for all of TDE when the marketing and promotion of his major label debut, *Follow Me Home*, fell short of expectations six years later. But with two hungry, talented young MCs on its roster, TDE decided to kill two birds with one stone: solidifying the strength of

the nascent label and announcing themselves to the East Coast on 2007's *No Sleep Til NYC*, a collaborative mixtape featuring K-Dot and Jay Rock.

What marks the immaturity of all these early efforts is a lack of any true auto-biography when compared to the literature-level memoir material of his post K-Dot career. Choosing to be known by his birth name in 2009 came with an elevation in the subject matter of his songs. Still, *No Sleep Til NYC* contains a scrap of something personal that connects the mixtape to *Hub City Threat* and *Training Day* on "It Ain't Hard 2 Tell": "For real kid, our uncle doing a thirteen-year bid/I pray to God he don't come out how he went in." The verse is an authentic moment of clarity placed direct-ly in-between surrounding fantasy rhymes about murder, smoking weed, and carry-ing a nine-millimeter handgun, the classic Nas single "It Ain't Hard to Tell" bumping underneath.

When Kendrick's parents first relocated to Compton from Chicago in 1984, an aunt helped them make the move. "My auntie Tina was in Compton," he once told *Rolling Stone*. "She got 'em a hotel until they got on their feet, and my mom got a job at McDonald's. Eventually they saved enough money to get their first apartment, and that's when they had me." Whether or not Tina is related to his uncle in jail is unknown, but it's probable. The first release under his own name, 2009's *The Kendrick Lamar EP*, contains "Uncle Bobby & Jason Keaton," a lament about incarcerated life and the prison industrial complex. The Polaroid picture used for the cover of *good kid, m.A.A.d city* shows baby Kendrick Duckworth on the lap of an uncle flashing a gang sign for the Crips, bracketed by another uncle and Kendrick's grandfather. All have their eyes hidden by black bars. On *Hub City Threat*, K-Dot brags on "Hovi Baby": "I'm still gettin' that cake, man/'Cause my uncle's still pitchin' rocks like a caveman." The reference is clearly to crack rocks. Come *Training Day*, he reveals on "I Feel It (Freestyle)": "Uncle Bobby's still incarcerated, Grandma died in Vegas/ Grandpa moved to Mississippi/I really can't tell if dude missed me/Probably stretched out on the floor, with an empty bottle of/whiskey next to his earlobe/More reason why my heart cold." He'll return to his grandfather's alcoholism five years later on "Swimming Pools (Drank)." *No Sleep Til NYC*'s "Preach" also denotes the men-tion of Sherane ("Champagne no, sweet Kool-Aid made by Sherane/Send her back to her boyfriend with cum stains"), the sexy inciting character of the whole *good kid, m.A.A.d city* narrative.

*No Sleep Til NYC* succeeds as another occasion to sharpen K-Dot's verbal technique, no more no less. In addition to Jay Rock, the mixtape also finds space for Compton MC Glasses Malone and TDE rappers Bo, Ab-Soul, and Punch. K-Dot doesn't even appear on several songs. Throwing back to the days when New York and Cali were the only rap zones that mattered, beat bedrocks from Doug E. Fresh and Slick Rick, A Tribe Called Quest and Big Daddy Kane get used. So do late-century classics from Mobb Deep, Jay-Z, and Biggie. By the end, K-Dot and Jay Rock can't resist tossing in some '90s left coast classics from Dr. Dre and Tupac. Mixtape DJ Big Mike hypes everyone's Myspace info, placing the project squarely in 2007. Like the collections that came before, *No Sleep Til NYC* is full of freestyle sessions meant to build on buzz. The buzz worked: that year, TDE signed Jay Rock to Warner Bros. Records.

Out of curiosity I took in a Lil Wayne show at the height of his 2009 love-him-or-hate-him infamy. Living in Paris at the time, I headed over to Le Zénith stadium to see nearly six thousand French fans bounce, sway, and rap along in broken English to "Lollipop," "Mrs. Officer," and other favorites from his latest triple-platinum, number one album, *Tha Carter III*. I'd already watched his progression from Louisiana's blinged-out Hot Boys as a teenager in the '90s to a phenomenally prolific solo star in the aughts. For years I'd made up my mind that his Southern-bred brand of hiphop didn't appeal to me, but that night, under the spell of his manic energy, the booming sound system and the crowd's enthusiasm, I got the point. But Wayne never needed

*"The Charles Hamilton come-out show: He had just signed a deal with Interscope, they gave him a big bag and all the music was poppin' for him. S.O.B.'s is like your coming out party. This particular night, young Kendrick was in the building. No one knows who this kid is. But Charles is a freestyler, so he is in the middle of the crowd with the mic freestyling. He hands the mic to Kendrick, who destroys him. The YouTube video is there. There's a part where Charles is looking at him like, 'Fuck, I shouldn't have ever handed this motherfucker the mic. 'Cause now, they're not gonna talk about me.' When he did that in 2009, I think that was the moment everybody was like, who is that?"*

—KEVIN L. CLARK

my vote. He'd soon have a record-breaking twelve songs on the *Billboard* chart at once, with a lush discography full of more mixtapes than official studio albums.

Months earlier, Kendrick made the rare move of dedicating an entire mixtape to another artist, crusading for Lil Wayne's bestseller with *C4* (as in *Tha Carter IV*, which Wayne himself wouldn't release for another two years). This is the MC listeners have come to recognize since, his execution finally equal to his ambition. Though the effort includes "Bitch I'm in the Club," a radio-pandering single he eventually knocked as his weakest song of all time, *C4* comes ever closer stylistically to the fully formed Kendrick Lamar on the horizon. (As Jay Rock's major label album came together, the TDE crew followed Wayne on tour through three states to secure a guest verse on Rock's single, "All My Life (in the Ghetto)." Wayne was on everyone's mind at the time, another reason for the *C4* homage.) "G Code" is the standout, built from the gospel-inflected, Kanye West–produced "Let the Beat Build" off *Tha Carter III*. K-Dot's rhyme flow is speedy, dexterous, assured. Instead of more cocksure battle rhymes, at twenty-one years old K-Dot gets nostalgic, coming up with some teenage tales from high school. His first foreshadows the entire plot of the upcoming *good kid, m.A.A.d city*: a homie on an "out of bounds" section of town for sex ("She had a fat ass and a brown Camaro, but it wasn't that fast, it was like a V6") who ends up on the wrong side of a .44 caliber handgun before it's all over. To paraphrase his moral of the story: fucking with scandalous hoes will get you killed. K-Dot's humor and storytelling powers prove he's come into his own.

Up until 2009, playing K-Dot had been like listening to a teenage Dylan imitate and approximate folk legend Woody Guthrie; *The Kendrick Lamar EP* is something more like *The Freewheelin' Bob Dylan*. No more mixtapes. K-Dot was born again as Kendrick Lamar, using his birth name for a fifteen-track EP that transformed the scrappy wordsmith into an artist. Extended-play (EP) records once were defined as albums that contained too few songs to be truly considered long-play (LP) records. But *The Kendrick Lamar EP* is a full-fledged, fully fleshed-out statement, containing more songs than hiphop classics like *Straight Outta Compton* and *Illmatic*. Autobiography, spirituality, honesty, and hiphop hubris infuse the EP with a distinctness previously unheard from Kendrick.

No longer jacking for other rappers' beats, most music comes courtesy of TDE in-house producers Sounwave, Dave Free, and King Blue, with one-offs from fellow rappers Black Milk and The Foreign Exchange, Jake One (of 50 Cent's G-Unit production crew), Wyldfyer and Pete Rahk. The resulting sound registers lighter than the prototypical booming G-funk beats pioneered by Dr. Dre or the trendy de rigueur sounds of modern MCs he'd been rhyming over on mixtapes. Many tracks would sit nicely on albums by Common or early Kanye; a listener might take Kendrick for a conscious backpack rapper. But they're the perfect complement here to his rhymes, which range topically from relationships ("She Needs Me"), consumerism ("Vanity Slaves"), and the prison system ("Uncle Bobby & Jason Keaton") to Christianity ("Faith") and individuality ("Let Me Be Me"). Independently released without a major record label, *The Kendrick Lamar EP* is still a stronger, more mature compilation than Jay Rock's Asylum Records debut *Follow Me Home*, also completed that year.[8]

---

[8] Warner Bros. put *Follow Me Home* on ice for two years due to internal personnel shakeups until TDE negotiated his release from the label. Strange Music finally dropped the album in July 2011.

With a chorus sampled from Télépopmusik's "Don't Look Back," the EP opens with "Is It Love." After six years of gangster posing, the song functions as the at-long-last revealed origin of Kendrick Lamar. He lets listeners all the way in for the first time. "While you were playing PlayStation, my pencil was erasing lines," he starts. The first verse takes us back to Kendrick watching *House Party*, eating Apple Jacks cereal, selling Sega games while his cousin sold crack, his uncles' drug dealing, and the abandoning of his basketball dreams. The final verse details all the frills of fame and fortune he hopes for as a rapper: expensive cars, Grammys, rings, chains, "me and Trump on golf courses." And even if the fates renege on all of that, he promises "I'll still give you Kendrick Lamar, this is me." Designating himself a good kid from the ugly city (harbinger of things to come, obviously), his transparency is bracing compared to the mixtapes.

"Good kid, mad city" comes up again on the following track, "Celebration," and much later on "Thanksgiving." This, Kendrick has decided, is his contribution to the culture as a hiphop persona: the good-hearted, well-intentioned son of unforgiving Compton streets, striving to stay true to himself in a ghetto life where trying to do so feels like making head against the wind. Given the treatment of African Americans in the United States, much less people of color around the world, his newfound vantage point is highly relatable.

"Welcome to my diary" he greets next on "P&P" (a treatise on the comforts of pussy and Patrón tequila), substantiating his claim for the rest of *The Kendrick Lamar EP*. His uncle Tony was killed outside a local Louis Burgers fast-food restaurant. His grandmother's death pains him. His grandfather's nickname was Cadillac ("Hello to my wittiness, I'm Cadillac's grandson," he says on "Trip"). Controverting old claims to Maybachs and Bentleys, on "Thanksgiving" he admits to "holding a cereal box instead of a Glock/in a 1992 Cadillac that I got from my pops." He distances himself from former idol Jay-Z twice: in a candid admission that he doesn't need a cosign from either Jay or Dr. Dre to succeed in hiphop, and in another confessional couplet on "Wanna Be Heard": "I used to wanna rap like Jay-Z/until I finally realized that Jay wasn't me." He admits to being broke more than once, hoping his rap ambitions flip his financial equation. "I wanna be a Trump/Donald that is," he raps on the bonus-track "Determined," his second positive reference to the future president.[9]

Kendrick Lamar came to Christianity in the parking lot of a Food 4 Less supermarket, baptized through a simple recitation of the Sinner's Prayer with a homie's grandmother out evangelizing for her faith. He dramatizes the scenario in a skit on *good kid, m.A.A.d city*. (Poet Maya Angelou plays the grandma.) But by *The Kendrick Lamar EP*, his unconventional baptism had clearly already happened. The musical bedrock of "Faith" is a midtempo, soulful sample of "Tired of Fighting" by the Brooklyn-based instrumental group Menahan Street Band. With an expressive hook by R&B singer BJ the Chicago Kid, "Faith" sounds as radio friendly as Kanye West's "Jesus Walks." But the track isn't a one-note testimony to Christ. The former K-Dot witnesses for his lord and savior in the first verse:

# "I opened my Bible in search to be a better Christian And this from a person that never believed in religion But shit, my life is so fucked up man, I can't help but give in."

By the end of his stanza, he exits the church service to take a phone call about the murder of a friend and loses his faith. He repeats the song's trick-ending narrative device in the second verse about a single black mother from Compton. She prays for better days only to receive a letter in the mail about losing her Section 8 status. "Faith" is a *Kendrick Lamar EP* standout, and he mentions God and his holy

---

[9] His respect for Trump as a symbol of wealth and success soured completely after his 2016 election. See "The Heart Part 4," "Black Friday" and "Wat's Wrong."

son elsewhere on "Wanna Be Heard" ("With Jesus Christ passion, I swear on the Bible"), "I Am (Interlude)," ("the passion of my Christ is in me"), and "Uncle Bobby & Jason Keaton" ("stay strong, keep your faith in God"). This is Kendrick's first album sounding as spiritually forward as Chance the Rapper or any given MC from the Christian hiphop genre.

Though I've never heard Kendrick cite Kanye as an influence, *The Kendrick Lamar EP*— thematically and sonically—has echoes of West's debut album, *The College Dropout*. If "Faith" stands in for "Jesus Walks," then Kanye's "All Falls Down" has a doppelgänger in "Vanity Slaves." (Kendrick's "Celebration" here even topically recalls the self-cheerleading of Ye's own "Celebration" from *Late Registration*.) He starts off the song wanting to zone out to the conscious jazzy boom-bap of A Tribe Called Quest, a surprise in itself from an MC who spent his mixtape career flag-waving for Tupac, Dr. Dre, and other West Coast gangster rap icons. Then he slowly unspools a meditation on how insecurity fuels materialism in the black community, railing softly but surely against designer name brands like Louis Vuitton and Gucci. He reaches back to the history of African-American slavery ("So blame it on the four hundred years we never saw/The reason why the next four hundred we gotta floss") and looks in the mirror at unconscious consumerism ("I care about my pride too much/If my clothes is new, if my ride is plush"). Then, just as Kanye points

*"Kendrick Lamar practices perfecting the delicate dance of posturing as an intellectual thought leader and evading the responsibility that comes with it. Sometimes by default, other times by deflection to the 'just an artist making art' stance. This is how he has evaded the controversies that come with a Kanye status, and circumvented the limiting 'conscious' title that comes with a Common status. He is chameleonic with his craft, during a time where rappers have more space to be so, and as a result, has operated with less restraint. He went from really good rapper to thought-provoking, liberation-anthem-making Pulitzer Prize winner in less than a decade. What saves Kendrick is the general consensus that he seems to have the capacity to keep getting sharper—that he can continue to hone every part of himself—from his pen game to his public persona."*
—IVIE ANI

the finger at himself at the end of "All Falls Down," Kendrick ends the track with a spoken outro asking TDE engineer Derek Ali for the nearest mall while they're out on tour in Idaho.

Did I say no more mixtapes? Imagine someone discovering Prince at the local movie theater in 1984 through *Purple Rain*, then finding out he recorded five other albums stretching back to 1978. Most music lovers outside the dedicated mixtape community had never heard K-Dot or Kendrick Lamar prior to *good kid, m.A.A.d city*. Many must have experienced the same wash of discovery as that newbie Prince fan when doing a deeper dive into Kendrick's discography after his Grammy-nominated major label debut. After *Y.H.N.I.C. (The Hub City Threat: Minor of the Year)*, *Training Day*, *No Sleep Til NYC*, and *C4*—plus his decision to rap under his birth name with *The Kendrick Lamar EP*—he released one last mixtape prior to signing with Dr. Dre: *Overly Dedicated*.

Though designated a mixtape, all the production is original[10]: mostly beats from Sounwave, Tae Beast, and Willie B. Kendrick has a penchant for the concept album, and in September 2010, *Overly Dedicated* marked his first attempt at one. Abbreviate the title and it's *O.D.* Squint closely and the mixtape's black-and-white cover reveals artists whose untimely passing was drug related.[11] Different tracks deal with addictions of various sorts. With references to the crack-era gangster flick *New Jack City* and the stoner comedy *Friday*, "Night of the Living Junkies"[12] overflows with drug allusions ("Bad bitches, crackheads, street niggas, crack hoes/This shit is so dope, you might wanna be my crack hoe"). And though the song harks back to the braggadocious K-Dot days, his level as a lyricist is clearly on a higher frequency all throughout *O.D.* The gimmicky, Afrofuturist love song "Alien Girl (Today With Her)" resembles the plot of that year's *Runaway* short film from Kanye, encountering a sexy E.T. who makes him admit, "I'm addicted, and you the drug/Cold turkey? No sir."

---

[10] Almost all. Opener "The Heart Pt. 2" stems from "A Peace of Light" by the Roots.

[11] The full list: Ol' Dirty Bastard, Pimp C, Michael Jackson, Jimi Hendrix, Bruce Lee, Kurt Cobain, Jim Morrison, Robert Johnson, Eric Snow, Dashiell "Dash" Snow and Sacer.

[12] Note the title's commonality with Public Enemy's 1988 crack cautionary tale "Night of the Living Baseheads." Both titles are takes on the 1968 horror classic, *Night of the Living Dead.*

Love addiction comes up again on "Opposites Attract (Tomorrow w/o Her)." Storytelling Kendrick evokes playwright Eugene O'Neill's The Iceman Cometh with his first verse, early evidence of the literary value of his lyrics. In an echo of that celebrated play's philanderer Hickey Hickman, the song starts from the perspective of a man who cheats on his doting partner precisely because she's so unconditionally loving. The second verse delves into emotional and physical abuse from her viewpoint, closing with the chanted chorus, "we hurt people that love us, love people that hurt us." Other songs in keeping with O.D. as a concept album include "H.O.C." (for "high on contact"), where he confesses to not being a marijuana smoker, and "R.O.T.C. (Interlude)," on which he contemplates shelving his rap career for drug dealing only to arrive at a moment of clarity courtesy of his "right on time conscience."

On "Ignorance Is Bliss," Kendrick goes back into K-Dot gangster mode again, spitting "the hardest shit you've heard from L.A. thus far" over a sample of D'Angelo's "Alright." The conceit is that the narrator knows not what he does, and therefore his ignorance is bliss. Kendrick has his cake and eats it, applying his elevated lyricism to the hard-core hiphop trope he left behind on his mixtapes. Later that year, the YouTube visuals for the song caught the eye of Dr. Dre, who reached out to Kendrick on the Independent Grind Tour with Jay Rock and Tech N9ne. With "Ignorance Is Bliss," he was officially discovered in a very real way, as his association with the legend's Aftermath Entertainment label opened the door to the evolution of his career.

Enter the beat switch. "P&P 1.5," his reprise of *The Kendrick Lamar EP*'s "P&P," turns the beat around midway through, with a nod to the chopped and screwed production of Southern hiphop in the song's second half. Another beat switch occurs on "H.O.C." Every Kendrick Lamar album to come will flaunt beat switches of their own, to the point where the maneuver has long become part of his signature sound.[13] As a technique, the beat switch in popular music can be traced at least as far back as 1969 on Sly and the Family Stone's "You Can Make It if You Try" but it's become a favorite trick of Kanye, Drake, and Kendrick in the '10s.

Jumping back to "P&P 1.5," it's also the first time that listeners hear Kendrick switch up his voice on an album-length project. (The non-album cut "I Hate You" marks the absolute first time, his 2009 musical hate letter to Death. In the third verse, Death responds in Kendrick's altered lower voice.) In part inspired by Prince and his high-pitch modulations (think "If I Was Your Girlfriend"), Kendrick once told producer Rick Rubin, "I've always been heavy on vocal tone and the way you manipulate your voice, because different tones for me just deals off of different expressions." With *O.D.*'s conceptual ambitions, beat switches, and voice manipulation, the mixtape sounds in retrospect like a musical sandbox for Kendrick to play around with ideas he'll masterfully execute later on *Section.80*; *good kid, m.A.A.d city*[14]; *To Pimp a Butterfly*; and *DAMN*.

---

[13] Other prime examples include "m.A.A.d city," "XXX," "Swimming Pools," "Sing About Me, I'm Dying of Thirst" and "DNA."

[14] *O.D.* opener "The Heart Pt. 2" also mentions Master Splinter, the rat sensei from the '80s comic book *Teenage Mutant Ninja Turtles* who gets referenced in a major way on *good kid, m.A.A.d city*'s "Sherane a.k.a. Master Splinter's Daughter." (Why is Sherane the daughter of Splinter? Because she's a hood rat.)

Rappers don't rhyme about coke anymore, rappers *are* Coke. I dreamed that line; it woke me out of bed in the middle of a night I should've already been finishing this chapter. The closest Kendrick Lamar has come to rhyming about coke appears on *C4*'s "Compton Chemistry," running down the elaborate process of cooking up cocaine into crack before the reveal: "You should thank me twice/Though you learned from a chemist who never moved a brick in his life." Coke rap was never the wheelhouse of either K-Dot or Kendrick Lamar, though he circulated mixtapes in the era when Young Jeezy and Clipse ruled that hiphop subgenre. Rappers certainly still rhyme about coke; see Pusha-T's *Daytona*. But the greater insight my subconscious stumbled onto concerns rappers as Coca-Cola.

As a rap artist, K-Dot was never a brand and couldn't have become much of one. Battle rappers, however talented, are as ubiquitous as soulful singers in black church choirs. Once Top Dawg Entertainment and their Compton-born signee came to that realization, Kendrick Lamar started rhyming about himself under his given name. In order to impact hiphop culture and the wider world at large as planned, K-Dot had to be reborn into a product that could be universally marketed and promoted (and identified with). Like Coke, sure, but also like N.W.A in all black with their L.A. Raiders caps, or Kanye in pink polo shirts and Louis Vuitton, or Nicki Minaj and her Jessica Rabbit body work. Like woe-is-me

*"The MC qualities that often get stamped as 100 percent Kendrick aren't always 100 percent Kendrick. Kendrick is an amalgamation of rappers who came before him. He has conglomerate qualities of rappers who preceded him—Busta Rhymes, Nicki Minaj, Lil Wayne, Kurupt, Tupac—who may have not had the same formula of success that endows him with this specific type of visibility. Whether he has studied any of them specifically or not, cultural influence sometimes supersedes intent. We've heard rappers do what he does: incorporate theatrics, contort their voices, animate their raps, assume different characters on records. But where Kendrick seems singular is in his multiplicity of labels. He can be 'conscious,' comical, whimsical, thoughtful, hard, vulnerable, 'woke' and turnt all at once, because we allow him to. Women, queer rappers, or any other marginalized community within hiphop have not been granted the same type of agency. What characterizes Kendrick's craft is its embodiment of liberation—he has the freedom to be whatever type of artist he wants to be, whenever he wants to be it."*
—IVIE ANI

**53**

Drake in all his patented pathos, Future's strip club aesthetic, or the oddball shtick of Tyler, the Creator. Good kid in a mad city became a slogan worthy of *Mad Men*'s Don Draper or, certainly, its own album title, a slogan as succinct as "think different" or "just do it."

From the Ronald Reagan era to the regrettable age of Donald Trump, the phenomena of personal branding trickled down from corporate America into the everyday parlance of popular Instagram models. The agitprop of Public Enemy and the preachiness of the socially conscious hiphop era that Kendrick Duckworth was born into in 1987 would be far too heavy-handed in the new millennium. But there have been many dashes of positive messaging in Kendrick's music ever since he started speaking for himself, as himself, representing his generation. On-brand for Kendrick Lamar is reaching anyone impressionable with the sound of his wide-reaching voice that if he can transcend his gang-infested, low-income hood then so can anyone. On-message for Kendrick Lamar is reaching back to similar communities with events like his annual Christmas concert in Watts with TDE or donating fifty thousand dollars to his old Compton high school. The good kid from the mad city created a synthesis of conscious East Coast–identified lyricism and hard-core West Coast brazenness that would've sat well with the seventeen-year-old who foolishly dismissed Eazy-E.

# Chapter 2

# Hood Politics

**1.**

Kendrick Lamar is in chains, shackled and shuffling. A four-man chain gang shuffles directly behind him, dressed in drab blue prisoner uniforms. Only blue jeans set Kendrick's uniform apart as he shambles his way to a microphone stand, center stage at the Staples Center arena in downtown Los Angeles. He lifts his chained wrists over the microphone mount, sweating, concentrated. Most of the audience at the fifty-eighth annual Grammy Awards waited all night for this moment. Kendrick leads the night's nominations, one nomination shy of the most (twelve) any artist has ever received in one year: the late king of pop Michael Jackson, in 1984. All eyes on him. Then he opens his mouth and lets loose.

"I'm the biggest hypocrite of 2015," he says, invoking his most controversial line that year. Terrace Martin cries through a saxophone to Kendrick's left, imprisoned onstage in cell block 29. He repeats the line, which slowly, dramatically unfolds into "The Blacker the Berry," the second single from his celebrated major label sophomore album, *To Pimp a Butterfly*. Trump hasn't yet been elected; still Kendrick seems to speak directly to the basest of his constituency among the nearly twenty-five million people glued to their televisions, tablets, and smartphones. He's under no illusions about the fake niceties of micro-aggressive racists and he lets it be known. He runs down all the hated features of his hair, his nose, his penis. He's aware of white supremacist plans for his community, their hatred for his culture. On the world's biggest stage for celebrating music, Kendrick indicts everyone with ill intentions toward his people in prime time, unapologetically.

The song ultimately trades in the same theme of racialized self-hatred as Harlem Renaissance author Wallace Thurman's 1929 novel, *The Blacker the Berry*. Where Thurman's book grapples with intracultural colorism, Kendrick charges whites revulsed by African Americans with hating the men in the mirror: "I know you hate me just as much as you hate yourself." But Kendrick doesn't make it to that verse onstage. Those who know the song know the indictment.

Instead, he stumbles off (unchained now) to another Grammy set—a blazing bonfire flanked by tribal dancers and drummers—and another song. As Kendrick relocates himself from the penitentiary to a place evocative of the Motherland, the music shifts to a single that wins both Best Rap Performance and Best Rap Song before the night is through. But Grammy-winning singles are far more common than anthems. Kendrick's millions of viewers that night necessarily include activists who spent their 2015 protesting against the wrongful deaths of Sandra Bland, Freddie Gray, and other victims of police brutality. The Black Lives Matter movement was new to the world, and "Alright" became as much a rallying cry for them at nationwide demonstrations as "We Shall Overcome" in the 1960s was for freedom fighters of the civil rights movement. Liberating himself to a free space in the mise en scène of the Staples Center stage, Kendrick appropriately launched into his widely adopted mantra of hope and perseverance.

The crowd of twenty-one thousand peers, celebs, and record industry insiders, all summarily impressed, rest in the palm of his hand. With the same affected limping gait, he shuffles away from his eight backing dancers to one last microphone stand. This song no one knows. Parts of this "untitled 05" version appear three weeks later on *untitled unmastered*, a new album of studio outtakes, with a subtitle suggesting he first created the track on September 21, 2014. "On February twenty-sixth, I lost my life too," he mentions early, jumping off from the death date of Trayvon Martin to unpack a song devoted to institutional racism as modern-day slavery. Again, no one yet knows "untitled 05." And so the audience, now much more hushed, pays especially close attention. He suggests meeting violence with violence. He makes organized religion sound ineffectual and impotent, embodying a character who finds more solace in a firearm and the bottom of a bottle. He wraps up the song with three mentions of HiiiPower, his self-created fledgling movement meant to encourage honor and respect in black communities.

The beat drops out and a new backdrop illuminates the stage: a continental outline of Africa, with COMPTON written dead center in Gothic lettering. Everyone leaps to their feet in a standing ovation, cameras capturing seasoned MCs like Common and Run of Run-DMC applauding. Grammy host and veteran rapper LL Cool J, visibly impressed, cuts to a commercial.

In the space of six minutes, Kendrick Lamar invoked the prison industrial complex, black activism, Pan-Africanism, systemic racism, and the legacy of socially conscious hiphop. By contrast, rap trio Three 6 Mafia used their moment before an even larger audience at the 2006 Academy Awards to perform "It's Hard Out Here for a Pimp," yet signified nothing outside the literal confines of the song. The comparison is perhaps unfair. But Kendrick's performance is a prime example of why he wears the mantle of Tupac Shakur, why he's widely considered the most political rapper in the modern-day pop culture cosmos.

Just as Kendrick can be said to exist in a post-gangster rap era, he also came to power in a hiphop era of post-political consciousness. He was in diapers when Public Enemy considered themselves the Black Panthers of rap, and KRS-One shot an album cover inspired by the legendary photo of Malcolm X guarding his window with an assault rifle. In the late 1980s, Rakim had only just raised lyricism in rap to new levels of complexity before P.E. politicized hiphop with their classic, paradigm-shifting *It Takes a Nation of Millions to Hold Us Back*. Full of references to black liberation icons like Louis Farrakhan, Assata Shakur, and Malcolm X over samples[1] collaged with a Romare Bearden–level attention to detail, the album kick-started a Black Power renaissance in the culture. Kendrick missed that wave of cultural nationalist rap that included P.E., KRS-One, X Clan, Poor Righteous Teachers, and Brand Nubian. But its legacy impacted his idol.

---

[1] Jesse Jackson and Nation of Islam minister Khalid Muhammad were two of the voices sampled on *It Takes a Nation of Millions to Hold Us Back*.

Tupac Shakur, raised by members of the Black Panther Party, brought their ideology to bear on record and in life. Fusing black consciousness with the gangster trope popularized by the likes of Ice Cube, Tupac embodied the enlightened outlaw. He shot at wayward police. He invented a nebulous Thug Life ethos to rally his listeners against white supremacy, the direct inspiration behind Kendrick's HiiiPower philosophy. He rhymed about police brutality, poverty, racism, female empowerment, drug addiction, and mass incarceration. And most importantly, to paraphrase Kendrick Lamar, he charismatically made it look sexy. Hiphop has been political as a culture since the heyday of one of its founders, Afrika Bambaataa. His Universal Zulu Nation organization helped squelch gang violence in the South Bronx back in the early '70s. Tupac wasn't going to be rap's last militant; the culture's activist roots run too deep.

Kendrick also grew up under the social justice of rap duo dead prez, the positivist rhymes of Common, the consciousness of Lauryn Hill, Talib Kweli, and Mos Def. But save for Lauryn, none of those MCs ever turned their political savvy into the type of commercial success Kendrick currently enjoys. His politics aren't perfect. His political education has been public, awkward, and thrust upon him to a large degree. But making the effort matters to him. What's most important to bear in mind is that he's a child of lower-income Compton, California, whose main focus starting from puberty has been to climb hiphop's highest heights, to fight his way out of poverty to stand beside his childhood rap heroes as a peer. Kendrick's varied viewpoints in the years since he's been elevated into a generational voice reflect the mercurial fluctuations of a heated debate in a black barbershop.

Dissecting Kendrick's performance at the 2016 Grammy Awards properly means presuming that he chose "The Blacker the Berry," "Alright," and "untitled 05" as songs that represented where he stood as an artist at that point in his career and delving deeper into why. Opening with "The Blacker the Berry," Kendrick presented himself onstage shackled to a chain gang, restrained with handcuffs. His band stood behind bars. Later that same year, director Ava DuVernay released the Netflix documentary *13th*, about the intersection of race, justice, and the prison system. Through his lyrics ("you made me a killer") and his appearance as a prisoner, he uses the Grammy platform to cause viewers to consider the institutional roots behind American imprisonment patterns. He'd long since recorded "Uncle Bobby & Jason Keaton" on *The Kendrick Lamar EP*, telling the stories of an uncle and a close friend from Compton who were both serving time. Bringing attention to the prison industrial complex isn't an agitprop pose for Kendrick; the issue hits way too close to home.

Seven months earlier in Cleveland, Ohio, a coalition of black community activist groups across the nation called the Movement for Black Lives convened their first official conference at Cleveland State University. The city became a flash point in November 2014 when police officers shot and killed a twelve-year-old boy, Tamir Rice, for playing in a playground with a toy pistol. The conference concluded without incident until its final day, when police stopped a fourteen-year-old for boarding a bus back to his hometown with an open container of alcohol. Soon officers were pepper-spraying the crowd, which had right away advocated for the rights of the teenage boy. An activist phoned the boy's mother, and she shortly rescued him from police custody. It was an exhilarating moment, like the drama-

*"I understand Kendrick to be an artist who both creates things that push us forward and also things that should give us pause, in terms of the way he understands. There's a lot of textures, from the sexism inherent in a lot of his work to the misogynoir to almost a more poetic, Bill Cosbyesque pointing the finger back at black people. And that ain't cool. At the same time, I think it's precisely because of what his music has allowed, what he has provided as an artist, that many people haven't disposed of him. I don't think enough of us held him to account. By 'us,' I'm speaking here of the progressive, black, left, movement community that rallied around 'Alright'—which might've also been our opportunity at that time and after to hold him to account for some of the shit that he spewed in his lyrics."*
—DARNELL L. MOORE

tization in director Spike Lee's *Malcolm X* when the Nation of Islam refuse to vacate the streets outside a police station until they assure the safety of an arrested black Muslim. The thwarted police harassment prompted over two hundred protestors to spontaneously erupt in song: "We gon' be alright! We gon' be alright!" The whole scene recalls another Spike Lee production, the music video for Public Enemy's "Fight the Power," where a political youth rally in Brooklyn transmogrifies into a block party. Black Lives Matter had found its anthem, common knowledge by the time Kendrick Lamar chose to perform "Alright" at the Grammy Awards.

Africa loomed as the final image of Kendrick's set that night, a superimposed COMPTON in the heart of the continent. Superhero movie fanboys already knew that Marvel Studios slated *Black Panther* for 2018 but couldn't have predicted its future as the highest grossing film of that year, much less that director Ryan Coogler would invite Kendrick to curate its Grammy-nominated soundtrack. *Black Panther: The Album* features Babes Wodumo, queen of the African electronic dance music subgenre known as gqom. Johannesburg rapper Yugen Blakrok and his Jo'burg brother Sjava rhymed alongside Kendrick on the album as well, the sound of Afrofuturist hiphop from Black Panther's fictional African nation of Wakanda made real. All that came later. When Kendrick connected his ancestral homeland with his childhood neighborhood, the motivation likely came straight from the same inspiration behind *To Pimp a Butterfly*: his 2014 trip to South Africa.

The *good kid, m.A.A.d city* world tour took Kendrick and his Top Dawg Entertainment labelmates Jay Rock, ScHoolboy Q, and Ab-Soul through sixty shows in fifteen different countries. On February 7, 8, and 9, the TDE team played Durban, Johannesburg, and Cape Town night after night. They tapped local South African MCs like Khuli Chana and Reason to open the sold-out dates on Kendrick's first trip to the continent. He stayed for a full week, visiting Nelson Mandela's cell on Robben Island. Inspiration from the trip poured into later songs on *To Pimp a Butterfly* like "Momma" (symbolic of the Motherland) and "Mortal Man" (which name-checks Mandela on its hook: "The ghost of Mandela, hope my flow stay propellin' "). Rap fanatics in the politically conscious era of the late '80s replaced gold rope chains for leather medallions inscribed with the African continent swinging around their necks. Kendrick missed out on that, but still found his own way to the idea of diasporic solidarity between Africans and blacks in America.

Connecting those dots may seem like a minor gesture, but what's ultimately in question here is the attention of his younger hiphop fans, who might suddenly take Pan-Africanism into consideration for the first time because Kendrick said so. Black Panther didn't coin the famous phrase "with great power comes great responsibility"; that was Spider-Man. But it's a maxim Kendrick takes seriously to heart. *To Pimp a Butterfly* comments several times on the conflict of misusing influence, the resentment over abusing power. As an avid Christian who's infused religious references into his music for years, Kendrick has never gone on record about how often he flips through the Bible. Still, the late Stan Lee (cocreator of Spider-Man, Black Panther and so many other Marvel characters) likely cribbed the idea behind that signature saying from the book of Luke: "From everyone who has been given much, much will be demanded; and from the one who has been entrusted with much, much more will be asked." Whether Kendrick has read the verse or not, he arguably lives by it. Planting seeds in the minds of impressionable viewers at the 2016 Grammy Awards is only one example.

# 2.

Kendrick opened his Grammy performance with "I'm the biggest hypocrite of 2015," a line that kicks off every verse of "The Blacker the Berry." The song, inspired from the start by the murder of Florida teenager Trayvon Martin, reveals its payoff in the final line: "So why did I weep when Trayvon Martin was in the street/When gang-banging make me kill a nigga blacker than me? Hypocrite!"

Controversy sparked immediately.

In a society riddled with so many police-driven atrocities against African Americans, the nightly news tends to distinguish these incidents with the most sound-bite-worthy details possible. Along these lines, the nation remembers Trayvon Martin by his Skittles and AriZona watermelon fruit juice, as opposed to the toy gun of Tamir Rice, or the Oakland train stop Fruitvale Station, where an officer killed Oscar Grant, or chokehold victim Eric Garner's dying words, "I can't breathe." On February 26, 2012, seventeen-year-old Trayvon Martin, visiting his father's fiancée in a gated community in Sanford, Florida, returned from a local convenience store when George Zimmerman—an older resident with an extensive history of alarmist 911 calls—started chasing him. The self-styled neighborhood watchman had already phoned the police, calling Trayvon "a real suspicious guy . . . up to no good or he is on drugs or something." The two fought, and Zimmerman shot the teenager dead. Trayvon Martin's murder and George Zimmerman's acquittal months later served as the inciting incident behind the #BlackLivesMatter hashtag and the internationally recognized social movement to follow. Even nine years later, hoodies like the sweat-shirt Trayvon had on that night are worn nationwide every February 26 by those who stand in protest against his senseless murder.

What Kendrick appeared to say in no uncertain terms is that the narrator of "The Blacker the Berry" is hypocritical for mourning the murder of Trayvon Martin when as an African American, he's committed murder against his own brother in the past. Essentially, the black-on-black crime of gang violence Kendrick raises causes him to think twice about his grief over Zimmerman's killing. Of all the issues he could have raised related to Trayvon Martin—the stand-your-ground law, inequalities in the criminal justice system—he instead suggests that black Americans consider their own culpability. His misstep was not well received.

Without meaning to, Kendrick played right into the hands of a right-wing mindset which believes that critiques against the larger (white) power structure cannot hold muster until blacks address intracultural ills within their own community. His thought process on "The Blacker the Berry" resembles the whole Don Imus controversy of 2007. Facing criticism of his racist on-air comment ("that's some nappy-headed hoes there . . . jigaboos") directed against the Rutgers University women's basketball team, radio talk show host Don Imus immediately deflected, claiming that worse language about black women flies around in hiphop lyrics all the time. MSNBC took him off the air for two weeks, but his non-apology set media think pieces in motion about the negativity African Americans critique from outside their community versus what they allow within it. Kendrick must have known his baiting coda was contentious when he wrote it. A conversation starter maybe, a jump-start for discussions about black self-annihilation. He didn't seem to realize how conservative and naïve his idea appeared. Defending his view months after releasing "The Blacker the Berry," Kendrick told MTV:

A few people think it's just talk and it's just rap. No, these are my experiences. When I say, "gangbanging made me kill a nigga blacker than me," this is my life that I'm talking about. I'm not saying you; you might not even be from the streets. I'm not speaking to the community. I'm not speaking of the community. I am the community. When I say these lines, it's for myself. This is therapeutic for myself because I still feel the urge and I still feel that anger and that hatred for that man next door because I gotta get a call knowing that somebody around the corner done did this to my partner . . . So when I say these things, it's therapeutic for me. It's making me remind that I need to respect this man because he's a black man, not because of the [gang] color that he's wearing.

So he was speaking for himself to himself then. His response to the internet storm around his politics seemed genuine, not TDE spin to manage a misguided idea. Kendrick Lamar, at twenty-seven, was not some liberal arts pundit with a doctorate in political science. No one disputes his irrefutable brilliance as an MC. But politically, he was coming into a very public learning curve like a Nascar driver flying down the Daytona speedway. A month before he sent heads spinning with "The Blacker the Berry," he conducted an equally problematic interview qualifying the murder of Michael Brown in Ferguson, Missouri.

The sound-bite-worthy nightly news detail attached to Michael Brown's murder, for those who may have forgotten him in the large inventory of cops murdering black men in America, is "hands up, don't shoot." On August 9, 2014, eighteen-year-old Michael Brown and a friend walked the streets of Ferguson after pocketing some Swisher Sweets cigars at a local convenience store. Officer Darren Wilson, a cop in an SUV, stopped the two. Brown may or may not have reached inside for the officer's gun; testimony is inconsistent. Whatever the altercation may have been, Brown ran, then turned back and started approaching the officer, very possibly with his hands raised. Officer Wilson shot defenseless Michael Brown dead, and the entire incident set off two weeks and two days of unrest—police militarization, riots, and protesting—that black activists remem-

*"I don't agree with Kendrick's sentiments around hypocrisy. I don't think we can understand intra-communal violence without understanding the context that it sits in. At the same time, there aren't good answers for why black people do bad things to black people. We shouldn't deny the existence of black people causing other black people harm because it interrupts clean-cut narratives around racial segregation and structural racism. I don't wanna do that either. But I think it is not hypocritical to be upset about the murder of Trayvon Martin by a wannabe vigilante who was self-appointed as a neighborhood watchperson to basically keep black people out of that community, even though he himself is not white."*
—ALICIA GARZA

ber as the Ferguson uprising. Come November, a grand jury did not indict Darren Wilson. Around the country, the fresh Black Lives Matter movement used "hands up, don't shoot" as a rallying cry, posing with arms raised like Michael Brown did the moment he was killed.

Talking to a *Billboard* writer in a California recording studio two months later, Kendrick offered this:

I wish somebody would look in our neighborhood knowing that it's already a situation, mentally, where it's fucked up. What happened to [Michael Brown] should've never happened. Never. But when we don't have respect for ourselves, how do we expect them to respect us? It starts from within. Don't start with just a rally, don't start from looting. It starts from within.

The shadow of respectability politics eclipsed Kendrick's reputation as a critic of white supremacy the day his *Billboard* interview appeared online, albeit briefly. Maybe we didn't know him the way we thought, some said. Others wondered if the success of *good kid, m.A.A.d city* had changed his hood politics. The self-critique of his own black community sounded too much like the tired old idea that African Americans have to bring their cultural values into harmony with America's superior mores in order to earn equal respect from the likes of the Ferguson police department. As if blacks don't already respect themselves. As if the mores of white America haven't been suspect, from as far back as the genocide of indigenous Americans to the 2020 police killing of George Floyd. Rapper Azealia Banks spoke for black Twitter and many others in toto that afternoon, tweeting that Kendrick's comments were the "dumbest shit I've ever heard a black man say," raising the generational effects of racism, poverty, and discrimination against people of color in this country before telling him, "speak for your fucking self."

Kendrick's self-defense came short and sweet months later, after the February release of "The Blacker the Berry" (with its attendant controversy) and the March drop of *To Pimp a Butterfly*. He told New York City's Hot 97 radio station in April: "I forgive them. Obviously, they don't understand where I come from. They don't understand what I've been through. They don't understand what I've done to my community that tore

*"I think Kendrick is exactly the type of person that I think needs to be organized into a movement for social justice. Because currently, where his politics stand don't actually lead us there. But he is such an important voice that I would say that he should be target number one for an organizing campaign."*
—ALICIA GARZA

*"It seems right to me that Kendrick is a person who will grow over time in terms of his political beliefs. Here is a person that at one point might say, 'Fuck the White House, I'm screwing the system,' and then find it to be an honor to attend and be in the White House to push for the My Brother's Keeper initiative. That's par for the course."*
—DARNELL L. MOORE

it down. For them to take my words out of context—yeah, I forgive them." Kendrick's absolution was certainly the most Christian thing to do.

Before turning the finger back on himself (and, by extension, the black community) through his *Billboard* interview and "The Blacker the Berry," his first major gaffe in respect to his personal politics involved dismissing the voting process back in August 2012. Promoting *good kid, m.A.A.d city* in dialogue with the conspiracy news site Truth Is Scary, Kendrick remarked:

> I don't vote, I don't do no voting. I will keep it straight up real with you. I don't believe in none of the shit that's going on in the world. You talk with me, you talk with me for hours because everything has a contradiction, everything is higher ranking and way beyond us, way beyond people. So basically, do what you do, do good with your people and live your life, because what's going on isn't really in our hands. If it's not in the president's hands, then it's definitely not in our hands. When I say the president can't even control the world, then you definitely know there's something else out there pushing the buttons. They could do whatever they want to do, we all puppets. Just play your cards right.

Playing devil's advocate, it's not terribly difficult to imagine why a young black man from Compton might not believe in the electoral process enough to exercise his fifteenth amendment right to vote. The U.S. Census Bureau says African-American voter turnout declined in the 2016 presidential election, from 66.6 percent in 2008 (when then President Barack Obama ran for reelection) to 59.6 percent when Hillary Clinton campaigned against Donald Trump. The Electoral College conundrum that favored Trump over Clinton, in spite of her winning almost three million more popular votes, underscored the drawbacks of representative democracy for millions of disappointed voters who actually made it to the polls. Like all politicians, Obama's to-do list of campaign promises went only partially fulfilled by the end of his eight years in office. The prison at Guantánamo Bay remains open. War in Afghanistan still continues. This may be frustrating for someone not fully versed in the checks and balances of government, or even for someone who is. But believing that everything is "not in the president's hands" is hardly an uneducated, misinformed, or conspiracy-theorist point of view. Deciding to rock the vote, to vote or die, even though the end result won't move the needle of progress as far as you want (if at all) is ultimately a deeply personal decision. Nearly half the eligible voters in the United States (46.9 percent) stayed home on Election Day 2016. When Kendrick Lamar said that he is the community, as the meme goes: he said what he said. No small amount of folks from his community feel like "what's going on isn't really in our hands," with justifiable reasons to feel that way. Disillusionment or nonbelief in our government hardly ranks as radical; Kendrick represents plenty of people in that regard.

Days after his Truth Is Scary interview, Kendrick backtracked on Twitter. ("And when you do VOTE. Just make sure it's 4 the right reasons. This way you won't point the finger at that black man like y'all did. Again.") When November 2012 rolled around, he told MTV, "I think I'm going to go ahead [and vote for Barack Obama], just because I cannot see Mitt Romney [winning]." He laughed. "I'll be on food stamps my whole life! I just don't feel like he's got a good heart at all."[2]

---

[2] Kendrick prefaced all that with a characteristic statement about self-reliance: "I think that's one of our biggest failures as a community, as a generation: not wanting to go out and do for ourselves, and to sit back and wait. And then when it doesn't happen, we point the finger. I think we just really need to take matters into our own hands. Uplift our community, put money back in our community and show these kids how there's something different."

Bob Dylan—nonpareil poet, Nobel Prize winner, universally recognized voice of the 1960s counterculture—emerged from the American folk music tradition. One could say Kendrick Lamar put a foundational brick into a new twenty-first-century subgenre of African-American music; I like to call it woke music. Social protest in rhythm and blues originates with Marvin Gaye and *What's Going On*, an album so out of left field for its time that Motown founder Berry Gordy felt skittish releasing it into the world of 1971. Never had a concept album touched on topics like war, poverty, racial injustice, even ecology, in the same soulful tones used in the R&B tradition. Gaye's masterpiece made possible all future full-length albums thematically looking through a political lens, from Bob Marley's *Exodus* to dead prez's *Let's Get Free*.

Black Lives Matter originated from the unrest in Ferguson following the death of Michael Brown and gave an activist voice to the racial profiling, cultural inequality, and police brutality of today. But just as the Black Arts Movement of the 1960s grew out of what poet Amiri Baraka, the Black Panthers, Malcolm X, and others called Black Power, Black Lives Matter emerged in tandem with woke music. As no one under a certain age needs to be told, to be woke is to be alert to society's injustices, racism specifically. Appropriately, woke music started with the soulful disciple of Marvin Gaye (and, for good measure, Prince): D'Angelo, and his comeback album after fourteen years of silence, 2014's Grammy-winning *Black Messiah*. His lyrical leitmotifs about war, social justice, love, spirituality, and the ecosystem mirror *What's Going On*, updated for the millennial age of social media and hashtags such as #BlackLivesMatter. "It's about people rising up in Ferguson and in Egypt and in Occupy Wall Street and in every place where a community has had enough and decides to make change happen," D'Angelo said in a statement when *Black Messiah* dropped.

One socially conscious album maybe means nothing, but at least three make a trend, and soon, more woke music followed. Solange released the feminist, for-us-by-us *A Seat at the Table*. With "Formation," especially its video, her superstar sister Beyoncé dipped in a pedicured toe. Her "Freedom" single totally qualifies, Beyoncé's *Lemonade* ode to liberation featuring Kendrick ("Stole from me, lied to me/Nation hypocrisy"). Janelle Monáe's "Hell You Talmbout" single chants the names of eighteen police victims, including Sandra Bland, Sean Bell, and Aiyana Jones. Childish Gambino's *"Awaken, My Love!"* challenged Kendrick Lamar's *DAMN.* for Album of the Year at the Grammys in 2018, on the strength of the ubiquitous single, "Redbone." (Singer Donald Glover's central hook commanded listeners to "stay woke!") But three months after *Black Messiah*, Kendrick released his own woke music classic, *To Pimp a Butterfly*. I talked to him about the connection between woke music and the Black Lives Matter moment in the summer of 2015. He said:

First, that is an incredible album, D'Angelo's *Black Messiah*. And it's a trip, because it took me nearly two years to create this record, without even knowing that [he] was on the same wavelength. For D'Angelo to drop out the blue and make a record like that, it was confirmation for me. 'Cause I was just wrapping up my project, and for him to do that, that was just confirmation. Of course it takes an incredible artist to do that anyway. He's been on that wave. But to hear that, for my generation it was definitely confirmation.

And it's only right, man. The times that we are in, it's something that you can only feel in the air. You don't even have to talk about it. You don't need the news or the internet to watch it. You can walk outside and just feel it. And these are the same times that I believe Marvin Gaye and them felt, just in a whole other generational perspective. He's been on that wave. And for me to know he's been on that wave, Marvin Gaye, and to carry on that type of legacy is only right. I am from Compton. I am from the inner city, the ghetto. And if I can use my platform to carry on a legacy and talk about something that's real, I have to do that, period.

*To Pimp a Butterfly* deals with the survivor guilt of Kendrick Lamar achieving his wildest dreams post–*good kid, m.A.A.d city* and coping with newfound role-model responsibility. His real life reflected the same continuing struggle. From 2012 to 2016, Kendrick evolved from not believing in voting to casting his first presidential vote for Barack Obama's second term to his own private meeting with the nation's first black president at the White House. Obama had already publicly singled out "How Much a Dollar Cost" as his favorite song of 2015 in the media. In January '16, Top Dawg Entertainment released a video of Kendrick shooting hoops on a basketball court with a younger black boy and putting his cultural weight behind Obama's My Brother's Keeper mentoring initiative.

As the Donald Trump administration came to power, Kendrick served his sharpest barbs against the new president on 2017's "The Heart Part 4."[3] Over a bed of backing tracks later revealed as separate songs from the future *DAMN.* album, he calls the politically inexperienced leader of the free world a chump, a punk. He critiques the Electoral College, raising the issue of Russian collusion with his election (an allegation investigated by special counsel Robert Mueller for most of the impeached president's term). TDE eventually removed the track from streaming services, with Kendrick later telling *Rolling Stone* he wouldn't rhyme about the president anymore:

> I mean, it's like beating a dead horse. We already know what it is. Are we gonna keep talking about it or are we gonna take action? You just get to a point where you're tired of talking about it. It weighs you down and it drains your energy when you're speaking about something or someone that's completely ridiculous. So, on and off the [*DAMN.*] album, I took it upon myself to take action in my own community. On the record, I made an action to not speak about what's going on in the world or the places they put us in. Speak on self; reflection of self first. That's where the initial change will start from.

---

3 "Donald Trump is a chump, know how we feel, punk/Tell 'em that God comin'/And Russia need a replay button, y'all up to somethin'/Electoral votes look like memorial votes/But America's truth ain't ignorin' the votes."—"The Heart Pt.4"

*"I think he's committed to male supremacy. But he's trying to figure out 'who am I' and 'who are we.' I think there's a thing we should also acknowledge while holding Kendrick accountable, which is that in the absence of a narrative of black men who are being kings and needing to be restored back to their rightful positions of power, what other narratives exist about black men in this country that are positive? I just don't think that there are any. And so while I want to hold Kendrick accountable, I also need to be able to say: 'Here's the alternative.' I think that's something I'm still working through too."*

—ALICIA GARZA

January 2019 made me feel ashamed for ever having reviewed an R. Kelly album, for ever lending him even that much attention as a cultural critic without using the opportunity to take him to task for the sexual abuse allegations trailing behind him much of his career. That month, the Lifetime network documentary *Surviving R. Kelly* completely exposed the singer's sexual, predatory, and physical abuse of teenage girls since the 1990s, with details that swayed R. Kelly apologists and provided receipts for others who'd merely dismissed him as a lewd pop-culture punch line. The six-episode series' guiding executive producer, dream hampton, told *The New York Times* she kept a guard posted outside her home all night long as protection from Kelly or any fans of the truly fanatical variety. *Surviving R. Kelly* spotlighted the decades-long research of Chicago music journalist Jim DeRogatis into Kelly's sex cult of barely legal women, their physical and mental abuse, and an abundant amount of out-of-court legal settlements. But hampton's televisual decision to center the voices of African-American women made the most damning case. The one takeaway that all black viewers knew deep in their bones: R. Kelly would've been imprisoned underneath a jail cell a long time ago if his victims had been underage white girls. American culture doesn't value or protect black girls; *Surviving R. Kelly* provided all the proof anyone needed.

The Cook County state's attorney's office of Illinois started investigating claims against Kelly after the series' airing. The grassroots #MuteRKelly movement, launched in 2017, picked up more momentum. Radio stations around the country removed the singer from their playlists. Recording artists who'd collaborated with him in the past—Lady Gaga, Ciara, Céline Dion, and Chance the Rapper among them—removed those songs from streaming services and issued public apologies. RCA Records finally dropped R. Kelly from its roster. And some celebrities (Erykah Badu, Kanye West) caught fire for defending him. At that point Kendrick Lamar's name entered the conversation.

Back in May 2018, Kendrick threatened to pull his music catalog from Spotify if they refused to walk back a new policy banning songs by R. Kelly and rapper XXX-Tentacion for "hateful conduct" and "hate content." Anthony Tiffith, CEO of Top Dawg Entertainment, told *Billboard*, "I don't think it's right for artists to be censored, especially in our culture . . . My whole thing with them was, we gotta fix this situation, and if it can't be fixed, then there's gonna be a real problem. We're gonna have to start pulling our music from the site." (At the time, XXXTentacion faced multiple felony charges for domestic abuse. In June 2018, assailants murdered the twenty-year-old MC in a robbery.) In the aftermath of *Surviving R. Kelly*, the social media hivemind recalled Kendrick coming to the embattled singer's defense and wondered why censorship outweighed all the black women calling R. Kelly a monster as the cause to champion. The TDE camp stayed silent.

The contradictory sexual politics of Tupac Shakur are legendary. Perhaps millions of women around the world felt empowered by the feminist-positive lyrics in singles like "Keep Ya Head Up" and "Dear Mama," or appreciated Tupac for centering their stories on "Brenda's Got a Baby" and "Me and My Girlfriend." The MC also served nine months in jail for sexual assault—a rape conviction leveled on him when he failed to intervene as members of his crew sexually violated a woman in a Manhattan hotel room against her will. More than any other rapper, Tupac posthumously served as a guiding light for Kendrick Lamar. Pac's influence shines through in Kendrick's objection to white supremacy, his consistent solidarity with the hood that birthed him, and the overtures to his female fan base.

With his light-skinned privilege, actorly good looks, and countless lovelorn appeals in his music, Drake makes a far more likely magnet for attracting female listeners than Kendrick Lamar, whose ears evoke Will Smith or Barack Obama; they stick out. He stands at five feet six inches short. His gap-toothed smile is charming, but far from the Hollywood veneers of other male celebrities. He spends far more time in the recording studio than at the gym. And yet he's still known for seductive lyrics exploring his heart and his sexploits on songs like "Poetic Justice," "She Needs Me," "For the Girlfriends," and my favorite, "LOVE.," along with plenty of others. More than Jay Rock, Ab-Soul, or ScHoolboy Q, the loverboy of TDE with the greatest concentration of women at his live shows is Kendrick Lamar, hands down.

But his sexual politics, as far as they can be figured out, raise questions. "A.D.H.D." dates back to his career as an independent artist (2011), and it is the only music visual he's released to date directed by a woman, Vashtie Kola[4]. Kendrick's videography includes over thirty different visuals. In a period when Ava DuVernay executive produces every episode of *Queen Sugar* for Oprah Winfrey's OWN network with all female directors, at a time when the Netflix superhero

*"Kendrick reads the world; he is an interpreter of the world. But he's particularly an interpreter of various aspects of black life and black urban spaces within white supremacist America. I was listening out for how the works that have been done for the Movement for Black Lives [impacted him]: the various messages about a type of expansive blackness that also includes safety for girls and women, and understanding that trans and queer folk are also pivotal to the movement, and understanding that this is not just about finger-pointing back at black people as problems, but a reevaluation of the ways that we exist in communities."*

—DARNELL L. MOORE

---

[4] In 2018, Kendrick reached a settlement in a copyright lawsuit by British-Liberian visual artist Lina Iris Viktor for copying her black-and-gold painting series Constellations for his "All the Stars" visual (directed by Dave Meyers and The Little Homies). Using the work of a female artist without her permission isn't a good look—especially for a male MC who, though largely seen as standing up for women, has almost never used female directors.

*"My first reaction was: who gives a shit about what Kendrick thinks I think about my body? Weighing in on what you think about my body is actually not helpful in a whole bunch of ways. You're setting the standards as opposed to me setting my own standards. At the same time, his music is not directed towards me. I think he's directing this conversation to other black men, and that's a conversation that I want to influence but I'm not a part of. In the same way that I would say I want my level of autonomy, I want him and other black men to have that level of autonomy so they can go at it with each other. Where I'm best served is to go at it with my sisters around shit we're dealing with."*
—ALICIA GARZA

drama *Jessica Jones* did the same to balance sexist inequities in television, it might be reasonable to expect more from Kendrick on that front, mainly because he records songs like "Keisha's Song (Her Pain)," a *Section.80* track fleshing out the backstory of a street worker with dignity and sympathy. Kendrick regularly presents himself as a feminist ally in this way, but the pose doesn't hold under scrutiny to any skeptic paying the slightest attention.

In March 2017, "HUMBLE." came under fire by those attentive skeptics. Calling for self-humility and the humility of hiphop competition, Kendrick's first number one single stands as one of the greatest in his catalog. The quip that put a target on his back this time sounds at first like an attempt to be progressive around beauty standards, but mostly ends up shallow and patronizing: "I'm so fuckin' sick and tired of the Photoshop/Show me somethin' natural like Afro on Richard Pryor/Show me somethin' natural like ass with some stretch marks." On cue, Blasian model Carter Kim struts through a before-and-after split screen in the "HUMBLE." visual, from a typically airbrushed video vixen look to parading a bouncy mane of natural curls and the cellulite of her backside. As the postmillennial court of public opinion, Twitter produced its own split screen of reactions. Many praised Kendrick for uplifting natural beauty, his obvious intent. But just as many others took a more critical tack.

**82**

Nothing underscores that Kendrick's social consciousness isn't sophisticated enough to extend to gender quite like "HUMBLE." Never mind that he says "bitch" forty times in the song, a term he uses liberally on all his albums (see "Bitch, Don't Kill My Vibe," etc.). Taken alone, Kendrick sharing his personal preferences about what turns him on is neither here nor there. But in light of his history of pandering and presenting himself as a Tupac Shakur–type advocate for women, his intention to gift some kind of broad-minded critique of beauty standards is clearer. And on that level, he falls short.

That's because Kendrick still sets the bar for ideals of attractiveness, for what's allowed and what isn't, in his backhanded thumbs down to hiding stretch marks and whatever else he personally doesn't consider natural. The problem in a nutshell is, who asked him? His "HUMBLE." verse brings to mind rapper André 3000 in an old OutKast song, flirting with a lover over wearing granny panties because he's not in the mood to see her in a G-string. Both MCs take away the agency of the woman involved while supposedly relieving them of the need to live up to an oppressive male-set standard of sexiness. But they do that by replacing one standard with another. Kendrick still dictates the conversation about what's hot and what's not, feeding the same vicious circle of patriarchal, heteronormative beauty ideals. That's not very humble.

*"We got this song. But were you listening when they said that trans lives matter? If you look around the Movement for Black Lives, you see that most of these folk that are leading are girls and women, and they're sex workers or cis or transgender folk, gender-nonconforming folk. What extent, if any, did that shape not just his lyricism, his artistry, but his music? I'm not certain. Maybe if he sat down with me, he'd say, 'I wasn't paying attention to that shit, I was in the studio creating art.' Or maybe he'd say, 'I have been impacted by it.' But I'm not certain I've seen that reflected."*
—DARNELL L. MOORE

Women never needed Kendrick's blessing to wear their hair natural, walk the beach showing their stretch marks, filter away cellulite in Instagram photos, do away with lipstick and eyeliner, or any other thing. It's not his place to say. On *Section.80*, "No Makeup (Her Vice)" poses the same problem. The twist ending there turns out to be that the woman with the makeup vice is hiding a black eye beneath all that concealer, the same street worker character from "Keisha's Song (Her Pain)." But the sentiment conveyed throughout the whole song is that Keisha's love for makeup (and, by logical extension, all women's love for makeup) reflects deeper insecurities about how she feels about her looks. "Don't you know your imperfections is a natural blessing?" Kendrick mansplains, all the while guiding her self-presentation based on what he personally finds attractive. Different song, same problem.

SZA, the loudest female voice in the TDE camp (if not its *only* female voice), unsurprisingly defended her labelmate (at least publicly) after the "HUMBLE." flap, to *Glamour* magazine: "How is that misogyny if he's supporting positive body image?" she asked. "I think that's so weird, and it's reaching. If you want to support women, you should support all shapes of women. I used to be two hundred pounds, and I have stretch marks all over my body. I find more comfort and solace with Kendrick reinforcing that I'm beautiful. I don't really feel anything misogynistic from that."

Far worse sexism has existed in hiphop. Comparably, Kendrick's chauvinism has nothing on Ice Cube mulling over kicking a pregnant woman in the stomach[5], or Snoop Dogg making light of gang rape on a hook[6], or Nelly running his credit card through the deep cleft of a woman's ass to watch it jiggle[7], or even Public Enemy judging women for watching soap operas[8] or dating white men[9]. His misogynoir pratfall on "HUMBLE." seems worse because he's a Pulitzer-winning intellectual who's supposed to be above such false feminism. He's been crowned with brilliance, very often deservedly so, but just as often his crown fits askew when it comes to womanism.

---

[5] "You Can't Fade Me" (1990)

[6] "It Ain't No Fun (If the Homies Can't Have None)" (1993)

[7] "Tip Drill" (2003)

[8] "She Watch Channel Zero" (1988)

[9] "Pollywanacraka" (1990)

Is Kendrick Lamar a hotep? Or at the very least, a fauxtep?

Making my way through middle school in the Bronx, I once knew a brother and sister whose father made a spectacle every parent-teacher conference. Their dad wasn't argumentative at all, he never raised his voice at the administration. But he was an African-American man who made a point of dressing in embroidered bou-bous, complete with knitted Kufi caps, to meet with the mostly Jewish faculty at our junior high every November. A committed Pan-Africanist, Mr. Adimu was all about the liberation of black folks. I almost took his daughter to prom eventually, and the library of black authors, black history books, and conspiracy theory literature in their apartment proved he was also committed to a revolution of the mind. (I never returned his copy of Harlem Renaissance poet Jean Toomer's *Cane*.) Mr. Adimu was the first person ever to greet me with an enthusiastic "hotep," the first to explain to me the word's ancient Egyptian meaning: peace.

Mr. Adimu passed away some years ago, and so has the cultural nationalist con-connotation of hotep ever since snark got a hold of it. Mention hotep now, and in most circles the assumed definition means different things, none of them peaceful. Ho-teps are black male supremacists, whose concept of black liberation excludes black women. A cartoonist would draw a hotep in dreadlocks wearing kente cloth with a homely white girlfriend on his arm. Their Pan-Africanism is narrowed by a shal-low historical perspective of the continent, usually limited to ancient Egypt (which they'll insist on calling Kemet, its original name). Hoteps' misogynoir often points the finger at black women, or white supremacy, for all the community's obstacles (but rarely capitalism and never patriarchy), absolving black men of any responsibility. Aside from their misogyny, they're also both homophobic and transphobic. And their conspiracy theories—like Beyoncé belonging to the Illuminati—get them dismissed by anyone with a modicum of common sense. I've never personally met a hotep, but though the characterization sounds harsh, they're out there.

Brother Adimu was a black liberation nationalist; he schooled me on hotep, but I never knew him to be a hotep. In deference to the likes of Mr. Adimu and his tribe in the black community, some prefer the term fauxtep, to make the distinction between African-identified freedom fighters and condescending, regressive, anti-intellectual, anti-LGBTQ misogynists.

Running down the different avenues of Kendrick Lamar's discography, his artistic exploration of contradiction comes up repeatedly. To paraphrase the MC from multiple interviews, contradictions and inconsistencies make us all human, and he loves to delve into them. He's been braggadocious to the nth power while telling MCs (and, subliminally, himself) to be humble, for only one example. Kendrick is large—he contains Whitmanesque multitudes, and intentionally so. When explored, his politics are more retro than backwards fauxtep. He may eventually catch up to the politics of Black Lives Matter, which adopted "Alright" years ago. But today

*"I think Kendrick has hotep tendencies. By 'tendencies,' the reason I'm making that distinction is because I don't get a sense that he's fully committed to it. I think he is someone who is looking for answers. Frankly, I'd say that our movements are responsible for going deeper with people like Kendrick, who has hotep tendencies, and really kind of doing the work to lovingly bring him into the right relationship with the complexity of who black people are."*
—ALICIA GARZA

there's no evidence his politics include a commitment to the freedoms of transgender and queer lives, which are so central to the Movement for Black Lives. The central message of his politics boils down to a black communal self-reliance rooted in the philosophy of Malcolm X.

Kendrick's response to *Rolling Stone* about the Trump presidency concentrated on strengthening the black community, with a message to focus on ourselves instead of misdirecting our energies outward. When cornered about voting years earlier, Kendrick downplayed the role of government in our lives and advocated empowering ourselves. His criticized comments over the murder of Michael Brown circled back to black self-respect. There's no evidence that Kendrick is a voracious reader. And yet the one book he's cited in interviews more than once is *The Autobiography of Malcolm X*. He's name-dropped the Islamic leader over and over in song, from "Imagine" to "HiiiPower" to 2011's "Little Johnny," which ends with Malcolm X speechifying about black independent thinking from a 1963 talk at the University of California, Berkeley:

> I think you will find, sir, that there will come a time when black people wake up and become intellectually independent enough to think for themselves. Then the black man will think like a black man and he will feel for other black people. And this new thinking and feeling will cause black people to stick together. And then at that point, you will have a situation where, when you attack one black man, you are attacking all black men. And this type of thinking also will bring an end to the brutality inflicted upon black people by [black people]. And it is the only thing that will bring an end to it. No federal court, state court, or city court will bring an end to it. It's something that the black man has to bring an end to.

On "Mortal Man," Kendrick questions, "How many leaders you said you needed then left 'em for dead?" before mentioning Malcolm, Martin Luther King, Jr., John F. Kennedy, Jackie Robinson, Jesse Jackson, and, finally, Michael Jackson. (He adds, "That nigga gave us 'Billie Jean,' you say he touched those kids?" as if Jackson's magical artistry should raise him above suspicion from accusations of child molestation that dogged his career since the '90s.) He throws back to a time when African Americans defended one another regardless of guilt or innocence because any justice in the white world was an oxymoron. No one would be surprised to hear of Kendrick defending Bill Cosby, like his defense of R. Kelly, over his imprisonment for sexual assault. Malcolm X's politics famously evolved after his estrangement from the Nation of Islam, and we can all most likely expect Kendrick Lamar's politics to evolve with time, maturity, and further exposure to the movement he's inspired through his music. He mentioned an eventual run for Compton mayor on "King Kunta," and we all assume he's joking. But with a reality TV star having served a term as president of the United States, all things are possible.

The morning after the 2016 presidential election, the *Norwegian Escape* cruise ship pulled out of port in Miami for parts unknown. Hundreds of thought leaders and roughly three thousand of their millennial followers set sail for "international waters" (as specified in the prep materials) to take part in Summit at Sea, an annual invite-only conference series for young professionals, spiritual leaders, and activists sharing ideas, funding projects, and creating partnerships to improve society.

For four days, attendees watched panel discussions and public conversations exploring themes like societal separatism, visionary social action, and the outer limits of human potential. Activists Patrisse Khan-Cullors and Erin Brockovich, Google billionaire executive Eric Schmidt, hiphop's Fab Five Freddy, Jermaine Dupri and will.i.am, TV producer Norman Lear, actor Daveed Diggs, poet Sonia Sanchez, and director Quentin Tarantino shared the wealth of their knowledge from Miami to the Bahamas and back. One night, attention from the young and sexy entrepreneurial elite centered on Kendrick Lamar.

Onstage with Tarantino and Citizens of Culture founder Maceo Paisley, the twenty-eight-year-old MC shared his thoughts on the creative process. "It's not about the equipment," he was quoted as saying, "it's about the hands working the equipment." Any other snatches of brilliance about brainstorming, eureka moments, idea incubation, or workflow will only be known by those who sat there listening. Summit at Sea prohibited social media and internet usage for the duration of the voyage, so there aren't a thousand shaky smartphone videos of the talk uploaded on YouTube to watch. In a way, it's the perfect metaphor to close on when it comes to Kendrick's genius. To say, "his brilliance is there, we just don't have evidence of it" is unfair. The virtuosity of his artistry is in full view from *good kid, m.A.A.d city* all the way through *Black Panther: The Album*. His presence among fellow thought leaders at Summit at Sea makes perfect sense; his invitation was no fluke. "As I lead this army, make room for mistakes," he told us all on "Mortal Man." With greater life experience and the passage of years, expect Kendrick to square his contradictions, maybe even building out a HiiiPower 2.0 ideology that'll surprise us all.

# Chapter 3

" i wasn't going to shoot you "

# Loyalty

Meredith Hunter rocked a lime green suit, black silk shirt, and a badass 'fro beneath a big-brimmed black hat to the most famous Rolling Stones concert of all time. In September of 1969, a month before turning eighteen, he'd loved all the hot fun in the summertime seeing Sly and the Family Stone, Thelonious Monk, Miles Davis, and more electrify a crowd of flower children and over-thirty squares at the Monterey Jazz Festival. A free Rolling Stones show over at the Altamont Speedway promised the same free-loving vibes, and so Meredith invited his girlfriend to the one-off December 6 performance. On the D-day, he borrowed the '65 Ford Mustang of his mom's boyfriend for the drive over and off they went.

Hells Angels biked around the crowd on Harley-Davidsons as security for the event, drunkenly laying down the law with fistfights and pool cues they wielded like billy clubs. The menacing atmosphere was no place for an unprotected young black man hand-in-hand with a blonde, miniskirted white girl. He circled back to the Mustang, popped the trunk, and retrieved a long-barreled .22 Smith & Wesson revolver to defend himself by any means necessary against the bearded motorcycle gang.

Finally the Stones arrived. Meredith climbed a speaker for a better view when the band hit "Under My Thumb," and while Mick Jagger shimmied and shook, a Hells Angel grabbed at his Afro, yanking him violently back down to the ground. Approached by a trio of bikers, he ducked into the massive crowd, his methamphetamine high all but blown under the circumstances. His fight-or-flight reaction quickly flipped in the opposite direction, and Meredith raised his pistol into the air in the general direction of the stage. His girlfriend reached for him, asking him not to shoot. With an arching sweep that so many would later say killed the innocence of the 1960s, a Hells Angel's arm came down on Meredith, knife in hand, and stabbed him six times in full view of both the audience and rolling documentary cameras.

"I wasn't going to shoot you," Meredith said with his dying breaths.

As he dropped to his knees, the biker—Alan Passaro—kicked him in the face repeatedly until other Angels also surrounded Meredith, and they all joined in to stomp the teenager to death. Another biker bashed him in the face with a garbage can. Passaro stood on Meredith's head while barking at a bystander, "Don't touch him, he's going to die anyway!" A Stones fan eventually lifted and carried Meredith to a Red Cross tent, but after rushing him to a nearby station wagon, nothing else could be done. His nose crushed, his stab wounds too severe, he passed away before doctors could helicopter him to a nearby hospital. Though the band stopped briefly, abandoning the show completely could've caused a full-scale riot, and so the young black teen likely died as the group soldiered through "Brown Sugar." The trial of Alan Passaro the following summer found the Hells Angel not guilty of first-degree murder, concluding he acted in self-defense—black lives considered no more valuable in 1970 than in 2021.

**Meredith Hunter,
may he rest in peace,
was a black hippy.**

Angela called work talking about A Tribe Called Quest at the Sound
Factory. So we met there. I saw Redhead Kingpin, Red Alert, and X
Clan popped onstage for a minute. The sound system was horrible.
They did "Bonita Applebum," "I Left My Wallet in El Segundo," "Can I
Kick It?," "Buddy" and "Description of a Fool." They're B-boys with
better samples.

—a journal, July 2, 1990

# I was there at the birth and the death and the rebirth of A Tribe Called Quest.

The tribe is called Quest, but I always called them Tribe. I stood in the sweaty audience of teenagers and twentysomethings as a college sophomore when Tribe released their debut album—*People's Instinctive Travels and the Paths of Rhythm*—and played downtown Manhattan's Sound Factory club. I wrote about it in my journal for my eyes only. Eight years later I sat in a record company conference room with Q-Tip and DJ Ali Shaheed Muhammad, the late Phife Dawg on speakerphone from Atlanta, for the interview that announced their breakup to the world. (Chapter seven of author Hanif Abdurraqib's love letter to the group, *Go Ahead in the Rain: Notes to A Tribe Called Quest*, is entitled "*The Source* Cover." That was my *Source* magazine cover. Their split moved a lot of us.) We reunited for the last time at a Sirius XM studio when Tribe came together again eighteen years later for one last album. Kendrick Lamar appears on that final record's "Conrad Tokyo," as big a fan as anyone.

Everyone's favorite band feels personal to them, and Tribe will always be one of my most favorite. Never was I not a fan of hiphop music growing up in the Bronx. But I was a skinny, shy, bookish teenager who resembled *Off the Wall*–era Michael Jackson. I couldn't rhyme or breakdance or deejay or tag graffiti. My black leather bubble goose down kept me warm during the same winter Run-DMC sported similar coats on the cover of *Raising Hell*, and we drank the same forty-ounce beer bottles of Olde English with our crews. But I wasn't tough like I imagined those kings of rock to be. I lived vicariously through LL Cool J, Public Enemy, even Beastie Boys, because I wanted to be like them and wasn't. With their caricatured, outsized personas, who could be? Then came the Native Tongues collective.

Yes, the Jungle Brothers arrived first, with khaki safari outfits straight out of 1980s Banana Republic and rhyming over funky samples of Sly Stone and James Brown. And they introduced Q-Tip on their album. But the first group from the J.B.'s loosely knit Native Tongues hiphop colony that truly looked like me (I didn't shop at Banana Republic) was De La Soul. Rappers Pos, Dave, and DJ Maseo dropped an album with a yellow Day-Glo cover (hot pink on the back) decorated with flowers, twice as many tracks as the average rap record, and nerdy skits as song segues. They sculpted their flattop Afro fades into layered, asymmetrical works of art. Contemporaries of N.W.A and Too Short, De La Soul didn't wear *The Mack* on their sleeves. They were fans of quirkier films like *Bloodsucking Freaks*. On their biggest hit single, the trio set the record straight early on that they weren't hippies, even while wearing daisy-printed shirts and peace sign necklaces. But the whole concept that black hippies could even operate within hypermasculine hiphop didn't exist until them.

A Tribe Called Quest appeared the next year, and to describe them in De La Soul's words: the trio wasn't hard, they were complicated. That is to say, they never seemed dangerous, they seemed like me. Me and a million rap fans just like me. I imagined that if any MC in hiphop loved, say, satirical newspaper comic strips like *Calvin and Hobbes* or *Bloom County*, Q-Tip would. The mixes on the Maxell cassettes I listened to on Bronx bus routes blended rappers Just-Ice, Sparky D, and Ultramagnetic MCs with my parents' older stuff—Miles, Sly, Hendrix, Grand Funk Railroad.

*"I think that Kendrick has a good combination of macro perspective and micro perspective. On Section.80 and* good kid, m.A.A.d city, *he's able to build out different characters. He does a really good job of world-building. So you get invested in these characters, you get invested in how Kendrick himself survives in this world. In Section.80, he's talking about a generation. On* good kid, m.A.A.d city, *he's talking about his neighborhood pretty much, and himself. On* To Pimp a Butterfly, *it's much more insular. He's basically trying to figure out his place in the worlds that he's just described after more or less making it out. It's an element of survivor's remorse, it's an element of social responsibility, it's an element of leadership."*

—WILLIAM E. KETCHUM III

Music from American 1960s counterculture, music I imagine Q-Tip knew too. Producing *People's Instinctive Travels and the Paths of Rhythm*, Q-Tip mined from the '70s with Lou Reed, Roy Ayers, Weather Report, and other artists people our age weren't really supposed to know. Tribe presented themselves in patterned dashikis with swinging leather medallions of the African continent. Phife and Q-Tip didn't pretend to murder gangstas; they lusted after Bonita Applebum instead. Like De La Soul, peace and love found its way into their material without sounding uncool.

The Native Tongues were black hippies.

In 2015 Pharrell Williams, whose voice reassures us on the chorus to Kendrick Lamar's "Alright," executive produced *Dope*—the teenage coming-of-age movie that helped make a star out of actress Zoë Kravitz. She played the unattainable love fixation of a black geek; watching her took me back to the first time I'd ever heard her name. I was already seventeen when *The Cosby Show*'s Lisa Bonet gave birth to Zoë. (Her mom was the love fixation of this black geek.) As Denise Huxtable, Bonet gave voice to a type of African American that pop culture hadn't shown us before. She wore a nose ring—a much bigger deal in the mid-'80s—and thrift store fashion; she was flighty. The *National Enquirer* at a local supermarket told me she'd named her daughter Zoë (as uncommon a name for a black baby girl in 1988 as Edith or Gertrude) and that the daddy was a biracial rock singer, with tattoos, locs, and a nose ring of his own, by the name of Romeo Blue.

Romeo Blue didn't last. By the time I floated over the audience in Doc Martens boots on a sea of upraised arms at a Lenny Kravitz show four years later, everyone knew his real name. And by then I'd zeroed in on Lenny as a poster boy for how to exist in the world as a black boho. I'd pierced my nose, grown my locs, gone under the needle at Fun City Tattoo. (Clearly none of this is radical anymore. These practices were the face tattoos, body piercings, and stretched earlobes of 1990. My grandparents weren't happy.) I listened to and loved CDs by Bob Marley, Led Zeppelin, John Lennon, and Queen because Lenny Kravitz interviews turned me onto them. It was a pose, and in college we were all posing as far as I was concerned. But black alternative culture, what would be considered the Afropunk aesthetic today, looked like my tribe. The costume felt less like dressing up and far more like stripping down. Hiphop was still there for me. But the world started feeling more like a place where I could show up at a Rolling Stones show and not get murdered for it.

*"It's a wonder none of the other Black Hippy members have broken out to being anywhere near Kendrick's orbit in terms of mainstream pop culture. They all construct thematically cohesive album statements that mark them as serious craftsmen, all worthy of cult followings. ScHoolboy Q's albums are full of songs that feel as if they're a tumble of the dice away from being a Song of the Summer, if not the whole Year. Jay Rock continues to make roads into the internal states of gang-banger with music that borrows from Southern fried soul, off-kilter melodies, neo-soul atmospherics, and industrial-strength gangsta rap alike. A case can be made for Ab-Soul's continued obscurity—he relishes in the eccentric and hermetic, stuffing his appearances with the cheeky and inaccessible. In many ways, Ab-Soul is exactly where he chooses to be."*

—KRIS EX

**Lenny Kravitz was a black hippy.
On a good day, so was I.**

Kendrick Lamar's inspirations have always leaned more toward the West Coast. Top Dawg Entertainment symbolizes his very own Death Row Records if we're analogizing from the wonder years that made Kendrick Duckworth first want to become an MC. And Black Hippy—the TDE supergroup featuring Kendrick Lamar, Jay Rock, ScHoolboy Q, and Ab-Soul—might embody his own version of Tha Dogg Pound (the Death Row duo of Kurupt and Daz Dillinger) times two. Had the Native Tongues called themselves Black Hippy instead, the sobriquet would have fit like a glove. Black Hippy has nothing to do with black hippies, and neither the Native Tongues nor Tha Dogg Pound hold all that much in common with Black Hippy.

For one, the quartet doesn't represent an alternative African-American lifestyle like early De La Soul or A Tribe Called Quest. One of De La's most famous lines, "Fuck being hard, Posdnuos is complicated," doesn't strictly apply to Black Hippy. The foursome reserves the right to be both hard and complicated. For another, Black Hippy resembles a twenty-first-century N.W.A far more than Tha Dogg Pound. Grouped altogether, they can appear as iconic as classic Eazy-E, Dr. Dre, Ice Cube, MC Ren, and DJ Yella from 1988. However. The Native Tongues never released a joint album. The hiphop collective stayed isolated to remixes and occasional guest appearances on one another's albums (most notably the monster De La Soul single "Buddy," with Q-Tip, the Jungle Brothers, Queen Latifah, and Monie Love on the side). The Black Hippy discography thus far consists of about thirteen "Buddy"-like posse songs to date, and they may never record an official, major-label studio album. I wouldn't even expect one.

Who is Black Hippy then? Like some hiphop Fantastic Four, these challengers of rap's unknown come with personalities as distinct as members of Wu-Tang Clan. Jay Rock is the straight-spitting (former) Bounty Hunter Blood from Watts; ScHoolboy Q is the (former) drug-hustling, Hoover Crip single dad from South Central Los Angeles; Ab-Soul is the conspiracy theorist mystic from Carson; Kendrick is the conscious renegade from Compton. Each MC explores himself so thoroughly on his own solo output that Black Hippy songs like "Rolling Stone" tend toward the playful. If they hadn't formed a group, TDE fanboys would've always fantasized over how these charismatic MCs would sound as a team. So they beat us all to the punch.

"We formed that in like 2009. When I was slacking on music and I was on selling Oxycontin, I decided to come up with the group. I figured if I wrote on one verse I would be straight. I figured that could work because I was too busy trying to make money. I figured I could just write a verse and they can handle everything else, so I figured let's just come up with a group. I always was just running with the name Hippy and Kendrick put the Black in front of it and we came up with Black Hippy. We did it to just fuck around. We did the record and everybody went crazy for it and then we just had to stick with it."

—ScHoolboy Q

# Jay Rock

Born and raised in Watts, Johnny Reed McKinzie Jr. was already two years old the month his future partner Kendrick Duckworth was born, four miles away, in Compton. The two are the oldest and youngest of Black Hippy.

Located in South Central L.A., Watts holds a particular place in the popular imagination of black folks. Fred G. Sanford and his son, Lamont, ran a Watts junk dealership at 9114 South Central Avenue on NBC's *Sanford and Son* from 1972 to 1977. One of the first television sitcoms to star African Americans, *Sanford and Son*—produced by the visionary Norman Lear—featured stand-up comedian Redd Foxx in his most well-known role. Based on the BBC's *Steptoe and Son*, the show brought Watts into American living rooms for thirty minutes every Friday night with a propulsive Quincy Jones theme song. A staple in my childhood TV diet alongside *Good Times* and *The Jeffersons*, *Sanford and Son* stands large in the collective pop culture experience of blacks from a certain time and place. Johnny McKenzie Jr. might've caught the reruns, but he certainly saw it. We all did.

What Watts also recalls is Wattstax: the 1972 benefit concert, the documentary film of the following year, and the 1965 uprising that made everything necessary to begin with. The Watts rebellion of August '65 escalated from a violent argument between police and Marquette Frye, a twenty-one-year-old black man pulled over for drunk driving. The community got word of police kicking Frye's pregnant mother on 116th Street and beating Frye. Mobs formed, throwing rocks and concrete blocks at arriving officers. Over the next six days, the National Guard and thousands from law enforcement sprayed fire hoses and engaged in brawls with the good citizens of Watts. Arson and looting of white-owned businesses went wild. By the end, thirty-four deaths and over forty million dollars in damages were reported. People moved out to other areas if they could. Four years later, Watts had the highest crime rates in California.

Memphis, Tennessee's renowned soul music label Stax Records organized a benefit concert, Wattstax, for the neighborhood at the Los Angeles Memorial Coliseum on August 20, 1972. Comedian Richard Pryor, activist Jesse Jackson, and a slew of 1970s musical talent—Isaac Hayes, the Staples Singers, Rufus Thomas, and the Bar-Kays included—created a concert that quickly became known (speaking of black

*"Jay Rock raps like a gangbanger who's surrounded by some of the best, most craft-centric rappers in the world and he doesn't want to let them down. His closest analog is Game, a fellow L.A. Blood likewise dedicated to a form of rap that hearkens back to impressing other rappers with old school wordplay. But where Game always feels like a bona fide rapper who bangs, Jay Rock is one of the very few rappers who has his feet solidly and equally planted in both realms. He experiments with flow, voices, attitudes, and modes in ways that most street-oriented rappers won't."*

—KRIS EX

*"Even though he has all his own music, I think Jay Rock's verse on [Kendrick's] 'Money Trees' really embodies what I expect from him. Just like from a street perspective, straightforward. He has a lot of bass and bounce to his voice, which makes him pretty versatile on just about anything."*

—WILLIAM E. KETCHUM III

hippies) as a black Woodstock. Public Enemy's *It Takes a Nation of Millions to Hold Us Back* held a crown as the greatest hiphop album ever made for years, and if you've ever heard it, then you've heard Wattstax buried in its mix of samples. Jesse Jackson exhorting "I don't know what this world is coming to" as he brought Stax quartet the Soul Children up onstage makes up the famed introduction to Public Enemy's "Rebel Without a Pause." A sample of the Bar-Kays' "freedom is a road seldom traveled by the multitude" opens P.E.'s "Show 'Em Whatcha Got," and a snatch of the Bar-Kays' "we're gonna get on down now" pops up in the bridge to P.E.'s "Night of the Living Baseheads." The *Wattstax* documentary is a time capsule and an African-American cultural monument, doubly so if one grew up in Watts like Johnny McKenzie Jr.

The Nickerson Gardens housing complex, two blocks from where cops attacked Marquette Frye and his mother, is where young Jay Rock grew up. Nas has Queensbridge; Jay-Z has Marcy Houses; Jay Rock has Nickerson Gardens, the largest public housing development west of the Mississippi. Named after William Nickerson Jr., the founder of Golden State Mutual Life Insurance, the housing project is mostly known for birthing the Watts Bounty Hunter Bloods. Crips and Bloods have feuded throughout southern California ever since 1969, spreading wide across the country to Chicago, New York City and beyond, with periods of peace and periods of conflict. MCs allegedly affiliated with the Bloods in their past include Game, DJ Quik, and Waka Flocka Flame; Kendrick Lamar's father and uncles were also reportedly in the Blood life. As a teenager at local Locke High School in the 2000s, Johnny McKenzie went Blood too.

At the time, gang injunctions in L.A. served as civil court orders restricting anyone listed on them from associating with friends and family in neighborhoods rife with gang activity. (In 2018 the American Civil Liberties Union won a lawsuit in California arguing against gang injunctions as unconstitutional.) Cops briefly jailed a teenage Jay Rock twice for violating the Nickerson Gardens' anti-gang injunction. Already known as a skilled battle rapper with a surprisingly gruff, husky voice in contrast to his lanky frame and chill demeanor, Jay Rock got targeted again: not by the L.A.P.D. this time, but by Anthony "Top Dawg" Tiffith. A hulking figure with criminal connections in his background (including his uncle Mike Concepcion, a founder of the L.A. Crips), Top Dawg finally cornered Jay Rock getting his hair cut on a porch in the projects to offer him the first slot in his newest music venture, Top Dawg Entertainment.

This was the year, 2005, that Jay Rock met K-Dot in the bowels of the House of Pain recording studio, in the back of Top Dawg's Carson, California, home. Their chemistry as a rap duo seems obvious in retrospect, but a series of Jay Rock mixtapes—*Watts Finest Vol. I* (2006), *Watts Finest Vol. II: The Nickerson Files* (2006), and *Watts Finest Vol. III: The Watts Riots* (2007)—came before their joint collaboration, 2007's *No Sleep Til NYC*. As the cornerstone foundation to TDE, Jay Rock unsurprisingly attracted attention from the record industry before anyone else. Top Dawg Entertainment made its first major-label joint distribution deal when Jay Rock signed to Warner Bros. Records imprint Asylum Records in 2007.

"All My Life (In the Ghetto)" signaled Jay Rock's arrival on mainstream urban radio in fall 2008. After following Lil Wayne's tour bus from city to city, the Houston MC (on the winningest of winning streaks at the time) agreed to lend some lines to the single. Jay Rock represented the first face average rap fans could associate with TDE through the visuals of "All My Life"—set, of course, in the heart of Nickerson Gardens. But the launch of his debut album, *Follow Me Home*, sputtered then stalled completely. Warner Bros. had a changing of the guard, replacing its current CEO with an exec who'd been leading the label's hiphop division. *Follow Me Home* collected dust while the company went through its backroom machinations, and when the corporate musical chairs started, Top Dawg negotiated Jay Rock off the roster. The way big business works, no new hires would want to score success with a rapper associated with the regime they replaced. Rather than watch *Follow Me Home* die a slow death lost in neglect, TDE partnered with a fellow indie label, Strange Music (founded by Missouri rapper Tech N9ne), and July 2011 marked Jay Rock's official coming out.

Very much a major label step up from his mixtape days, *Follow Me Home* featured will.i.am, Chris Brown, Rick Ross, and Lil Wayne, as well as Kendrick Lamar on the record's only other single, "Hood Gone Love It." Multi-instrumentalist Terrace Martin, responsible for so much of Kendrick's *To Pimp a Butterfly* four years later, produced both "Just Like Me" and "M.O.N.E.Y." A straightforward hard-rock MC, Jay Rock comes witty ("Easy money fool's paradise/I roll with it like a fool with a pair of dice") with tales of growing up as a product of Watts and Nickerson Gardens. Alongside the high-profile guest appearances, Ab-Soul lends hooks to "Life's a Gamble" and "No Joke." ScHoolboy Q drops a line on "Bout That." TDE had released Kendrick's *Section.80* debut album two weeks earlier; for listeners, he was a relative newbie with the superior CD, still showing up for hooks on *Follow Me Home*'s "They Be On It" and "Code Red." Black Hippy united for the first time on "Say Wassup"—a posse cut that solidly holds its own but honestly isn't even a highlight of *Follow Me Home*. Critics loved the album.

At the time of his sophomore follow-up *90059*—named for the zip code of Watts—*good kid, m.A.A.d city* and *To Pimp a Butterfly* had already wowed the streets, the radio, the Grammys, and the pop populace. TDE learned from the trials and errors of launching Jay Rock's career and applied those lessons to Kendrick with wild success. Less of a traditionalist West Coast gangster rap album than *Follow Me Home*, *90059* takes chances with weightier, varied music and more detailed lyrical tones. By 2015, listing Kendrick as a collaborator could sway newcomers into a download, and so here he is on *90059*'s first single, "Money Trees Deuce" (itself a sequel to their *good kid, m.A.A.d city* team-up, "Money Trees") and the standout Black Hippy formation, "Vice City." Aside from detours like the social media dis "Telegram (Going Krazy)" and the *Silence of the Lambs*/Hannibal Lecter influence on both the album cover and its title track video, Jay Rock mostly stays in his lane here.

Kendrick Lamar rose as the superstar of TDE between *Follow Me Home* and *90059*. He dominated the 2016 Grammy Awards with a climactic, political performance of "The Blacker the Berry" and his anthemic "Alright" and five overall wins, taking nearly as many nominations as *Thriller*-era Michael Jackson. That same Monday night, paramedics hospitalized Jay Rock after a motorcycle crash cracked his pelvis and broke his left leg.

The most famous motorcycle accident in music history has to be Bob Dylan's crash of 1966. He didn't tour for eight years afterward, and the downtime shifted the whole evolution of his songwriting. Though Jay Rock is no Dylan (if I were to compare any of the Black Hippy crew to the legendary songwriter at all, it would be Kendrick), he experienced similar musical growth following his accident. When *Redemption* appeared in 2018, his subject matter had widened, becoming autobiographical even beyond his formative years in the crucible of Nickerson Gardens projects. Unlike TDE's independent *90059* release, Interscope Records partnered with the label for *Redemption*, and the deeper pockets may have made possible appearances by Future, J. Cole, and James Blake. But surviving the bike crash is what finally gave Jay Rock a deeper backstory to mine from, especially on the title track, in which he pictures his funeral in an alternate reality where he didn't survive.

On his official Facebook page, Barack Obama cited "Wow Freestyle" (a Kendrick collaboration) as one of his favorite songs of the year. "King's Dead," his swaggering trap masterpiece with Kendrick and Future, won Jay Rock his first solo Grammy for Best Rap Performance. He also charted on *Billboard*'s Hot 100 singles chart for the first time. It's all as if *Redemption*'s "Win"—full of "Gonna Fly Now (Theme from *Rocky*)"–like bombastic horn blasts—manifested his longtime intentions in full.

# SCHOOLBOY Q

Black Hippy wouldn't exist without Quincy Matthew Hanley. The concept grew out of his insecurities as an MC; he hoped that the three other rappers would do the heavy lifting in that regard. In time, ScHoolboy Q grew into the MC most likely to rival Kendrick in popularity and eventual success out of his entire crew.

Born on a military base as an army brat in the west Germany spa town of Wiesbaden, Quincy Hanley came into the world as the son of divorced parents. His mother relocated them to Houston, Texas, for three years before settling in California: 618 Hoover Street in South Central L.A. (His father remained enlisted.) Hanley's formative years involved playing football from the age of six, joining the 52 Hoover Gangster Crips at twelve, writing rhymes at sixteen, and selling weed, crack, and Oxycontin while holding down a 3.3 grade point average at Crenshaw High. (Director John Singleton made his alma mater famous in *Boyz n the Hood*.) Like Kendrick Duckworth, Quincy Hanley was a scholar, hence the "schoolboy." Like Johnny McKenzie, Quincy was a gangbanger—as a Hoover Crip, hence the stylized capital H's in "ScHoolboy" and all his various song titles ("THat Part," "Break tHe Bank," etc.). Also like McKenzie, Hanley got locked up. At twenty-one, police arrested him for his part in a home invasion about which he's never gone into heavy detail. He served three months. Unlike Jay Rock and Kendrick, Quincy Hanley attended college(s): Glendale Community College, Los Angeles City College, Los Angeles Southwest College, and West Los Angeles College, where he played football for the Oilers.

He's sly, he's a party boy, he's a scoundrel. We want to like ScHoolboy Q. He impersonates Elon Musk smoking marijuana in the "Numb Numb Juice" visual and we laugh. Video vixens on the beach bump and rub their bikini butts against his head in the "Man of tHe Year" video and we laugh harder. His daughter, Joyce Hanley, also softens his image, humanizes him. Born in 2010, she shows up in several of his visuals, and the *Oxymoron* album features her on its cover: three years old, scowling in her daddy's trademark bucket hat. As a personality, ScHoolboy Q has the charisma to match his expertise as a rapper more than any other Black Hippy besides Kendrick Lamar.

The cliché metaphor for superhero-obsessed hiphop culture casts Anthony Tiffith as the Professor X of TDE, the father figure organizer who collected everyone

*"ScHoolboy Q is an incredibly decep-
tive rapper; his flows and shortened
sentences speak to so much. An erratic
denseness permeates his work in a way
that allows you to enjoy his voice as
a sound but will pull you deep into a
broken underworld when you begin to
pay attention."*

—KRIS EX

together to hone their superpower (emceeing) at
his own school for gifted youngsters. Encountering TDE for the first time sets the stage for each
MC's origin story, that moment their mutant
abilities start to manifest. Of all the Black Hippy
quartet, ScHoolboy Q joined the group last. (Like
Marvel Girl then . . . Let's drop the metaphor.)
Already friends with twenty-year-old Quincy
Hanley, recording engineer Derek Ali first
brought him to the House of Pain studio in late
2006. Terrence "Punch" Henderson, TDE's president, told him to jump in the recording booth
for a song Jay Rock and Ab-Soul were working
on. The team continued to invite him back as his
skills kept improving. Two years later, ScHoolboy
Q officially made the cut.

Per usual, TDE pumped out free mixtapes to
seed the market: *ScHoolboy Turned Hustla* (2008)
and *Gangsta & Soul* (2009). But *Setbacks*, his 2011
debut album, proved the label might be a dynasty
in the making. Copious references to hash, marijuana, and alcohol threatened to establish him
as Fratboy Q, but at least his brand was crystal
clear. ScHoolboy Q parties. Black Hippy may
not have been aware of the murder of Meredith
Hunter at that Rolling Stones concert. But TDE
in-house producer Sounwave samples that era's
psychedelic rock staple, "Time of the Season" by
the Zombies, for a Black Hippy bop called "Rolling Stone." Kendrick Lamar adds verses on four
different songs. He tries convincing Q to drop

**114**

hustling drugs for hiphop on "Birds & the Beez"—in March of that year, police arrested him for marijuana possession at Austin's SXSW music fest. And "Live Again" ranks as my favorite ScHoolboy Q track, the one I can listen to on an infinite loop riding around on New York City transit. With Kendrick and young Brooklyn rapper Curtains, Q goes off over tried and true drums from Barry White's "I'm Gonna Love You Just a Little Bit More Baby" and a squealing sax, about the desolation of the streets ("Looking at the sky, hoping a light would shine/Daylight savings time all the time on this block of mines").

What makes Kendrick Lamar the most universally appealing Black Hippy also makes him one of the most universally appealing rappers in pop music: he makes personal experiences relatable on a macro level. The titles of *DAMN.* tracks are universal themes like "LOVE.," "LUST.," "FEAR.," "PRIDE.," and "LOYALTY." His partners in Black Hippy will probably never reach the rarefied heights of Kendrick or Jay-Z or Kanye West. Not because of talent; they all emcee way better than Kanye. But because braggadocio and better living through chemistry and gang-life survival don't resonate as deeply as love, lust, fear, pride, loyalty. They occasionally touch on these things too, but not like Kendrick does.

ScHoolboy Q seems more competitive with Kendrick than anyone else in his crew. *Oxymoron* was his first release to follow the widely acclaimed *good kid, m.A.A.d city*, and Q bragged to the media that he had no choice but to create his own classic after Kendrick laid down the gauntlet. He failed to understand that the story of a good kid in a mad city, of a good-natured heart at odds with violent circumstances, goes back to *The Godfather* or *West Side Story* or Shakespeare or the Bible. *Oxymoron* knocks hard. The Grammys nominated it for Best Rap Album. But Q still hasn't mastered the concept album like Kendrick, and *Oxymoron* doesn't try to transcend standard rap tropes enough to break through a higher ceiling of popularity.

Autobiography is still a great place to start though. Q mentions growing up with roaches in his breakfast cereal more than once on *Oxymoron*, like on the memoir track, "Hoover Street." He cracks his diary wide open on "Yay Yay" too, where he recalls growing up on Figg Street, his mother working overtime, the curfew imposed by his grandma, and why he sold crack and Oxycontin. He carries over a love of

*"All these different artists on TDE, they feel like they could be . . . I don't wanna say 'extensions of Kendrick,' but it feels like Kendrick took the best parts of them. Ab-Soul is sort of the weirdo of the crew. Kendrick has some of the same eccentricity as Ab-Soul. 'Ab-Soul's Outro' on Section.80, I think really embodies the synergy that TDE has more than just about anything that TDE has ever done. He sums up the essence of Section.80 in one song, down to referencing certain characters, down to referencing what the album is about. His rapping ability is just as strong as anybody in TDE, damn near anybody in rap in a lot of ways."*

—WILLIAM E. KETCHUM III

Portishead from his 2012 sophomore set, *Habits & Contradictions*: sampling the moody English band's "Undenied" on "Prescription/Oxymoron" like he borrowed the group's "Cowboys" for his gangster tale, "Raymond 69." His clipped style of rhyming evolves into more sophisticated couplets from *Habits & Contradictions* to *Oxymoron*. But the *Oxymoron* album isn't his *good kid, m.A.A.d city*, not in the way Q might've hoped. He's just not the overall conceptualist that Kendrick is, and that's okay.

In 2016 ScHoolboy Q's *Blank Face LP* received the same Best Rap Album nod as *Oxymoron*. (Q lost to Chance the Rapper's *Coloring Book* that time and Eminem's *The Marshall Mathers LP 2* the first time in 2015.) Lush with guest verses from veterans like E-40 and Tha Dogg Pound, plus the likes of Vince Staples, Anderson .Paak, and Kanye West, one of the greatest voices of his generation gets relegated to a chorus ("By Any Means") and two hooks ("Black THoughts" and "Overtime," which Kendrick also produced). It's the ultimate sign of ScHoolboy Q's evolution as a confident, masterful MC. The one Black Hippy who formed the group to cover up his own short-comings is the same one who steps the furthest outside of his camp as an individual these days.

Rapper Mac Miller became a valued friend over the course of Q's career and died in September 2018 of an accidental drug overdose. But his death doesn't lend any gravitas to 2019's *CrasH Talk*. Though Q delayed the release of his fifth album five months out of respect for Mac's death, his rhymes make no mention of him. (In the booklet to *CrasH Talk*, Q writes, "A song or an interview won't explain How much of a brutHa u was.... love u and r last convo was all I needed, tHanks for everytHang.") With light singles like "CHopstix" and "Floating," and using golf games as therapy, he preferred to let the good times roll.

# AB-SOUL

True, Ab-Soul looks like the sixth member of Bone Thugs-N-Harmony. His albums have sold the least and he comes up the shortest where his partners' radio hits and Grammy accolades are concerned. The esoteric nature of some of his lyrics make him the hardest to understand, and sometimes get the best of him. But make no mistake. Ab-Soul is not the U-God of Black Hippy. (No disrespect to U-God.) Lyrically he's closer to RZA: conspiracy theories, cryptic spirituality, occult references. Without a doubt he's the one most likely to name-drop Rastafarian messiah Haile Selassie, the mythical lost city of Agartha, and Marilyn Manson's favorite Satanist, Aleister Crowley, in his rhymes. Ab-Soul is the one black hippy of Black Hippy.

Herbert Anthony Stevens IV was born in L.A. but spent the first four years of his life in ScHoolboy Q's native Germany until his mother split from his Army-enlisted father. The two relocated to California, to his grandmother's house in suburban-ish Carson. His paternal grandfather, Cletus Anderson, owned Magic Disc Music—a popular record store with an affiliated Magic Disc Records indie label. Anderson produced local acts like the Most Requested Rhythm Band and Captain Rapp during the 1970s and '80s. Another of his labels, Saturn Records, released Ice-T's first single, "Cold Wind Madness." Grandpa Anderson also co-owned V.I.P. Records over in Long Beach, where director Fab Five Freddy set the video to Snoop Dogg's first single, "Who Am I? (What's My Name?)."

Young Herb Stevens spent his time working a register at the store with his mom, shooting basketball, playing Nintendo, watching cartoons. He sold CDs nearly every day, but when he turned nine, Bone Thugs-N-Harmony went number one with their requiem for mentor Eazy-E, "Tha Crossroads." (He'd died of AIDS complications at thirty.) For Herb, it was the rap song that served as a gateway drug for everything else hiphop had to offer. Later that year, Tupac Shakur also died after a drive-by shooting in Las Vegas. Serving all the mourning music fans passing through Magic Disc Records opened a window into the uniting power of music that he'd never looked through before. Then tragedy struck his own life.

At ten years old, Herb Stevens was hospitalized for the treatment of Stevens-Johnson syndrome, a skin condition transmitted by viral infection or medications like sulfonamide antibiotics. Symptoms include high fever and other flu-like reactions. The thin skin of his lips blistered, peeled, and regrew much darker (a condition he pokes fun at with the title of the very best Black Hippy posse track, 2012's "Black Lip Bastard"). His eyes sealed shut for two months with blistering and swelling, causing a light sensitivity he still moderates in adulthood with omnipresent black sun shades. When he emerged on the other side of recovery, he entered hiphop in a different way. Not as an aficionado, but as a practitioner.

At twelve, Ab-Soul wrote his first verse ever over the backdrop of Twista's "Emotions" and never stopped. Teenage Mark Spears, a cousin of an early rapping partner, created some original production for him with the MTV Music Generator program on his PlayStation. (Spears later joined Top Dawg Entertainment as in-house producer Sounwave.) As a fifteen-year-old on BlackPlanet, the proto-social media platform of the late '90s, he started "keystyling": typing out freestyle lyrics in online "textcee" battles against other young keystylers. Advanced placement classes eventually awaited him at Carson Senior High School, but by graduation, only two local community colleges accepted him into their institutes of higher learning: Harbor College and El Camino College. After less than two semesters, a bachelor's degree ceased to be the life goal; Herb Stevens had already leaned completely into Ab-Soul.

*"It's impossible to separate the* To Pimp a Butterfly *effect from the butterfly effect. Meaning: there's no way of telling if the other members of Black Hippy would have bigger or smaller marketplace footprints without Kendrick Lamar. Is Kendrick's success the halo which shines on them or the spotlight keeping them out? Is Kendrick as viable as an MC to so many different subsets of rap fans without his proximity to the unadulterated hood gazes provided by Jay Rock and ScHoolboy Q? Does Kendrick push himself to the outer limits of vocal choices without ScHoolboy Q's squawking aggressiveness and Ab-Soul's dense lyricism? Without Kendrick, is TDE just a group of really good rappers that would languish underneath consistent accolades of being underrated?"*
—KRIS EX

**121**

Prior to TDE, Ab-Soul had started making other alliances. He'd signed briefly to another indie label, StreetBeat Entertainment, as a member of Area 51. Another early clique called themselves the Notch Boyz. But when Sounwave, his old homie from the '90s, brought Ab-Soul by the House of Pain in 2006, Punch Henderson quickly added him to the TDE roster to start recording some mixtapes. The label's experience partnering with Warner Bros. Records for Jay Rock taught them some valuable lessons: signing with majors isn't the endgame, it's just the beginning; and the responsibility of building buzz rests with TDE, not Warner Bros., Interscope, or whoever else. To that end, mixtapes are essential. *Longterm* arrived in January 2009, followed by *Longterm 2: Lifestyles of the Broke and Almost Famous* a year and a half later, the first half of a proposed four-mixtape project. But in 2011, Ab-Soul felt prepared for his first official debut album.

*Longterm Mentality* preceded superior albums like Kendrick Lamar's *Section.80* (by three months) and ScHoolboy Q's *Setbacks* (by six months), yet Ab-Soul already considered himself the Black Hippy underdog. "T.D.U.D." stands for just that—Top Dawg Under Dog: "You would have thought I was infatuated with being underrated instead of renowned/Got me feeling like King David before the crown," he rhymes. "Almost There" reprises the same theme: "I know exactly how it is to feel like no one cares/About the hard work you put in, but who said life was fair?" Kendrick shows up on the bridge to "Hell Yeah," and also "Moscato," Ab-Soul's sex-and-wine celebration that's a topical retread of Kendrick's "P&P" ode to sex and Patrón tequila from *The Kendrick Lamar EP*. Most Black Hippy team-ups come last on their albums, and here it's the so-so "Constipation." With *Longterm Mentality*, Ab-Soul was only clearing his throat.

The masterpiece of his discography to date is *Control System*. This seventeen-song set reveals Ab-Soul the thinker. The cover of the album mixes the Judaic Kabbalah tree of life and its ten divine powers (loving-kindness, wisdom, and understanding among them) with the Christian fish symbol, Ab-Soul's name in the center. From this album forward, the Jesus fish becomes Ab-Soul's logo. He introduced *Control System* puffing out his chest with the "Black Lip Bastard" single, but the album is far more layered. "Motherfuck the government, motherfuck the system" are the first lines out of his mouth on "Bohemian Grove," a song that ends with a conspiratorial speech about Americans being enslaved through taxation. Ab-Soul and ScHoolboy Q attack the Stop Online Piracy Act on "SOPA," a bill introduced in 2011 to criminalize unauthorized streaming of copyrighted content with up-to-five-year prison sentences. "Showin' Love" finds him "pissing on the Declaration of Independence." Like the contrast between K-Dot and Kendrick Lamar, the Soulo of *Control System* barely resembles the so-called soul brother number two of *Longterm Mentality*.

"My enlightenment's the ancient Chaldeans/Penetratin' America's culture to its very being," Ab-Soul rhymes on "Beautiful Death." What exactly about these early Mesopotamians helps him critique Americana is never made clear, but it sounds deep. Ab-Soul exposes the hypocrisy of the country's moral fortitude at different points, mentioning Casey Anthony (a young mother who controversially got off scot-free after allegations of murdering her baby daughter) and Amber Cole (a fourteen-year-old girl whose viral oral sex clip set off an internet debate about sexual promiscuity) in "Beautiful Death" and "Double Standards," respectively. There's plenty here. He casually comes for Jay-Z on "ILLuminate." He flirts with a radio-friendly Drake flow on "Empathy." He shares murderous thoughts against police ("who just locked up my partner"), a preacher ("for miseducating the people"), and God ("for placing me 'round all this danger") on "A Rebellion." Kendrick Lamar, far more popular by now, raps on "ILLuminate" and the Black Hippy remix of "Black Lip Bastard," but it hardly matters. *Control System* is the Ab-Soul show, and he'd created the most masterful TDE concept album until *good kid, m.A.A.d city* dropped five months later.

Ab-Soul dedicated *Control System* to "the beautiful soul of Loriana Angel Johnson aka Alori Joh." The original angelic voice blessing TDE tracks with an added gloss of soul until Solána Rowe aka SZA filled the role, Alori Joh was Herb Stevens's longtime girlfriend. A vocalist from Carson, she sang on early Kendrick Lamar, ScHoolboy Q, and Ab-Soul tracks, releasing her own *The Love Religion* EP two years before her suicide. The twenty-five-year-old singer leapt from a radio transmission tower in Compton in February 2012. Ab-Soul soldiered on, but her death is mourned on songs recorded in her memory, like *Control System*'s "The Book of Soul."

Released four years later, *These Days . . .* took a welcome autobiographical route: "my girl died and I lost my mind" ("God's Reign"); "when my grandpa died, I broke down and cried" ("Stigmata"). Kendrick gets cathartic too on "Kendrick Lamar's Interlude": "I seen a dead body at five and that shit made me traumatized." But overall, things just don't cohere quite the way they did on *Control System. These Days . . .* reveals Ab-Soul the overthinker, a trend that worsened considerably with his fourth album, *Do What Thou Wilt.*, which qualifies as the worst Black Hippy album of them all. Mentions of planet Nibiru, the genealogy of Isis, the middle-Earth kingdom of Agartha, the philosophy of occultist Aleister Crowley . . . It's all far too much, especially when the music doesn't make you overlook the excess. Black Hippy's black hippy went full conspiracy theorist, but his lyrical skill never degenerated. Meaning that with the right hit, all will be forgiven.

It's four thirty in the morning and I just finished a dream about Q-Tip. He turned the key in the door of the northeast Bronx apartment I grew up in, the one I haven't seen since my mom moved out in 1990, the one that appears in my dreams a lot. Whatever midnight marauding he's been up to is over for the night. He warms us up some sushi in the oven (weird, since sushi is eaten cold) and we talk about Dilla's *Donuts*, and other things escaping my mind even as I write this. Eventually we get to my bedroom, and my hill of vinyl albums. I start crate-digging for the two records I've always wanted him to sample: John McLaughlin's slow, funky guitar build-up on "Honky Tonk," from the Miles Davis double album, *Get Up with It*; and Nicky Hopkins's opening piano trill on the Rolling Stones' "Monkey Man," off *Let It Bleed*. They're my father's albums that I grew up with, songs I know he must know and appreciate too. Even in my dreams.

I can never find the albums; I never did clean my room. Instead I wake up and get back to this book.

I don't dream of celebs often, even celebs I've met before. But my little emotional memory processor conjures Q-Tip because of what his group once meant to me as an identifiable mirror of the culture into which I was born. I was nineteen when I stood in the crowd watching A Tribe Called Quest drop their low-end in New York City for the first time live. There's a whole generation of millennials who've grown up on Kendrick's music, and the music of Black Hippy, for over a decade now: from MP3 files of *ScHoolboy Turned Hustla* on DatPiff to the Pulitzer-winning *DAMN.* on Spotify. Kids dreamed of making it out of their hoods with K-Dot mixtapes as their personal soundtrack, and he means even more to them than this Gen X dreamer.

Crews aren't what they once were in hiphop. A Tribe Called Quest belong to a bygone era. I don't expect to see a future Black Hippy project any more than I expect one from, say, the loosely knit Odd Future. Solidarity exists nowadays between MCs on the same label—like Nicki Minaj, Drake, and Lil Wayne on Cash Money, or J. Cole trying to launch careers on his own Dreamville label. True groups, even supergroups like Wu-Tang Clan and G-Unit, have disappeared. More money to be made solo, obviously, with fewer egos. The surrogate family atmosphere that posses provided for one another comes from the greater collective these days, a larger movement like TDE on a whole.

**126**

I wanted to end this by tackling black entrepreneurship, showing how Black Hippy excavates its own culture as a means of realizing the American Dream, with TDE following the template laid down by Death Row, Def Jam, all the way back to Berry Gordy's Motown. How corporatizing hiphop on their own terms pours profits into their own pockets, the originators and creators of the music and the culture. Those efforts have landed Kendrick Lamar on the cover of *Forbes*, not just the freshman class issue of *XXL*.

But dreams are much stronger than anyone's annual gross profits. So consider instead the good kid from wherever his mad city happened to be, waking up in the dead of night in his middle age after imagining Kendrick Lamar in his hardscrabble childhood home. Then rolling over to spoon his wife before the kids wake up, deeply grateful for how he got there for a few seconds before falling back into a deep sleep.

Chapter 4

# All the Stars

Hiphop of the '80s deserves its own alternate history. Down a divergent wormhole of some other space-time continuum, mainstream pop catches on to the Bronx-born subculture instantly. Indie label Sugar Hill Records never needs to bring acts like the Sugarhill Gang to *American Bandstand*; major labels like Polygram, Columbia, and RCA Records jump on board from the beginning. Any executive who ever calls rap music a passing fad gets fired immediately, from "Rapper's Delight" forward. At the turn of the decade, Busy Bee and Spoonie Gee sell millions of albums in the *Billboard* top ten right alongside Pink Floyd and Journey. In this timeline, where hiphop swallows pop culture whole from day one, the 1980s become a different-looking ten years indeed.

The Johnson Publishing Company, founder of *Ebony* and *Jet*, creates a black-owned monthly magazine devoted to urban music—rap, rock, reggae, rhythm and blues, funk, jazz—called *Shine*, dedicated to covering the music within the larger context of American pop culture. *Shine* launches in September 1980 with Grandmaster Flash and the Furious Five gracing the inaugural cover, photographed by Gordon Parks. The next three covers feature Bob Marley, Bad Brains, and the Cold Crush Brothers. When they consistently outsell *Rolling Stone*, publisher John H. Johnson turns the magazine into a biweekly. *Shine* gets showered with national magazine awards, helping push hiphop even further to the front and center of American culture, expanding the boundaries of the mainstream forever.

The Treacherous Three and Kurtis Blow score rap's first two Album of the Year nominations, but Run-DMC finally win the Grammys' highest award for their debut album in 1984. The self-titled *Run-DMC* trumps albums by Prince, David Bowie, Bruce Springsteen, and Cyndi Lauper for the prize. No one considers this an upset. The Grammy committee establishes rap categories as early as 1980, but rap albums consistently take the top Album of the Year honor all decade long: Run-DMC's *Raising Hell* (1986); Eric B and Rakim's *Paid in Full* (1987); Public Enemy's *It Takes a Nation of Millions to Hold Us Back* ties with N.W.A's *Straight Outta Compton* (1988); De La Soul's 3 *Feet High and Rising* (1989). Because they're pop albums. No biggie.

Hiphop galvanizes the youth vote nationwide, turning the Rainbow Coalition of Jesse Jackson into a substantial voting bloc that sweeps him into office in 1984, defeating Ronald Reagan in a landslide. As the first black president of the United States, the right reverend invites the Fat Boys to perform at the inaugural ball. (The trio's custom tuxedos are designed by Dapper Dan.) In our reality, President Barack Obama hosted Kendrick Lamar, Common, Rick Ross, Snoop Dogg, and Jay-Z at the White House. But President Jackson rolls out the red carpet for hiphop decades earlier in this timeline, inviting Rakim, Just-Ice, Big Daddy Kane, KRS-One, and Roxanne Shanté to break bread in the Oval Office during his first term. Gun-control measures passed by the Jackson administration end up saving the lives of DJ Scott La Rock and thousands of other victims of gun violence.

I enjoyed my teenage years of the '80s just fine, but this Earth Two 1980s was off the chain. In 1985, a black American microbiologist unjustly murdered by the L.A.P.D. in our reality for bumping Lovebug Starski too loud in his kitted-out Volkswagen Jetta instead lives on to worldwide acclaim, pioneering bone-marrow transplants that cure AIDS patients of the HIV virus. In the decades to come, millions (including rapper Eazy-E) never die of the autoimmune deficiency disease. The biggest hit of Michael Jackson's post-*Thriller* career comes with "Crack Kills," the most popular track on 1987's *Bad*, featuring Run-DMC. Condé Nast Publications awards Rakim the cover of *Vanity Fair* magazine in '88 and still comes off as late to the hiphop party. The Universal Zulu Nation eradicates gang activity in nationwide black neighborhoods with its four-point plan of peace, love, unity, and having fun;

the Bloods, Crips, and Gangster Disciples fade away just like the Black Spades and Savage Skulls of the '70s. On and on to the break of dawn.

The '80s, alas, didn't happen like that. Hiphop wouldn't break through the pop stratosphere once and for all until the '90s. Dr. Dre, Snoop, 2Pac, Biggie, Jay-Z, DMX, Salt-N-Pepa, Lauryn Hill, the Fugees, Master P, OutKast, and others sold so many millions more than rappers like Kool Keith or Dana Dane could ever have imagined ten years earlier. Will Smith and Queen Latifah earned Oscar nominations in Hollywood, and MCs signed endorsement deals galore with multinational companies. Your grandmother in 1988 would never have heard of MC Lyte; she certainly would have heard of Lauryn in '98.

Where am I going with this? Kendrick Lamar didn't spring full-blown from the head of the pop gods; he started as a scrappy teenage MC in the Compton hood. But he definitely sits on a throne of that particular Mount Olympus nowadays. It takes more than sheer force of will to scale that mountain. How did he evolve from the mixtape K-Dot of *Training Day* and *Overly Dedicated* to the Kendrick Lamar of *Vanity Fair* and *Rolling Stone* covers, Taylor Swift and U2 collaborations, White House visitations, and a Pulitzer Prize for music?

That ascendency started with the '80s. But not in the way you'd expect.

The title of Kendrick Lamar's debut album, *Section.80*, stands for two things. Section 8 status sounds as familiar as government cheese to anybody who's grown up in lower-income American neighborhoods. The Housing Act of 1937, Section 8, authorizes rental housing assistance to landlords on behalf of tenants who earn below a certain annual income. Amendments passed since then stipulate that households in the Section 8 Program pay around 30 percent of their rent; the remainder is satisfied with money from the federal government. (And for the record: rectangular blocks of processed cheese doled out to food stamp recipients and needy Americans on welfare, from World War II to the early '80s, were known as government cheese. In the Bronx, we'd toss slices onto grilled cheese sandwiches and omelets for months.) *Section.80* stands for the poor who are ten times more underprivileged than those who live under Section 8 status, as Kendrick's parents did for years.

The title's other meaning is a direct reference to the 1980s, of which Kendrick lived through a total of two and a half years. *Section.80* mentions "the dysfunctional bastards of the Reagan era" and "the children of Ronald Reagan" on songs like "Ronald Reagan (His Ills)." But the actor-turned-president left office less than two years after Paula Duckworth gave birth to baby Kendrick. Arguably far more to blame for the governmental policies of his youth were '90s presidents George H. W. Bush and Bill Clinton. Born in June 1987, Kendrick Lamar qualifies as a millennial all the way through, a child of the 1990s more than anything. But on Kendrick's first official album, "section 80" also stands for the generation born anytime during the 1980s, regardless of all the demographic subsections dreamed up by data strategists. Still, as a concept album, *Section.80* doesn't really deal with this demo much beyond scant references to crack babies, ADHD, and Reagan name-drops. Kendrick may indeed be millennials' champion MC ("People say I speak for Generation Y/Why lie, I do"), but the conceit doesn't hold *Section.80* together as well as his future concept-album ideas.

Top Dawg Entertainment released *Section.80* in July 2011, following an EP and five mixtapes dating back to 2003. Kendrick turned twenty-four that June. The universal props *Section.80* received from critics and the blogosphere turned him into an underground overnight sensation eight years in the making.

The day of its release, a tweet appeared from @drdre: "Everybody go download @kendrick_lamar's #Section80."[1] On the Independent Grind Tour with Jay Rock and Tech N9ne, Kendrick sat in a Chili's Grill & Bar in Kansas City, Missouri, in early 2010 when engineer Derek Ali got a phone call: by way of Eminem manager Paul Rosenberg, Dr. Dre had seen the video of "Ignorance Is Bliss" on YouTube, and wanted to speak with him. That *Overly Dedicated* mixtape track led the young gun MC to record with the West Coast kingmaker weeks later. *Section.80* dropped the following summer with the cosign from the ultimate cosigner. The N.W.A producer—unanimously considered the Quincy Jones of hiphop—brought Snoop Dogg,

---

[1] That was then, this is now: @kendricklamar is his verified Twitter handle these days.

Eminem, 50 Cent, and Game to the highest level of the genre. He was poised to work his magic all over again for this Compton MC from his high school alma mater, who was clearly just as much of a lyrical technician as the others. Their association leaked to those in the know, and even though their collaborations were held until the next album, *Section.80* dropped with Dre's seal of approval (see Twitter). Consider Kendrick signing with Dr. Dre's Aftermath Entertainment as the first domino setting off his pop culture dominance.

My minority view positions *The Kendrick Lamar EP* of 2009 above *Section.80*, but let's look at the bright spots of his first major record. In the spring of 2019, I taught a college course at New York University's Clive Davis Institute of Recorded Music in downtown Manhattan. (NYU hired Q-Tip, Spike Lee, Zadie Smith, and other well-known adjuncts in the past; I felt in great company.) Thirty students signed up for Kendrick Lamar and 21st Century Hiphop in Cultural Context, and when they explained why on the first day of class, someone mentioned his undying love for *Section.80*'s "Rigamortus." Sampling a spirited three-piece brass section from modern jazz drummer Willie Jones III's "The Thorn," the song features Kendrick racing through two verses of rapid-fire lyrics about how he's killed your

*"I think of To Pimp a Butterfly as his greatest overall musical achievement. I don't care about us getting validated by the Pulitzers. We don't need that. Kendrick did more for the Pulitzers than the Pulitzer did for Kendrick. That being said, I could listen to DAMN. and see how the mix of lyricism, poetry, storytelling on a track like 'DUCKWORTH.,' I can definitely see how that's something that they could apply their metrics to and see as really easy to reward. So I think it makes sense for DAMN. to get it. Even if that's not the album I would have rocked the most."*
—JAY SMOOTH

**139**

favorite rapper. Kendrick and producer Willie B designed "Rigamortus" to leave listeners' heads spinning, and it does its job. Impossible to follow unless your ears have been attuned to hiphop forever like most of the *Section.80* generation, "Rigamortus"[2] is the direct opposite of a catchy, radio friendly unit shifter.

First honorable mention for the album's best tune goes to the J. Cole–produced lead single, "HiiiPower." One song earlier, Kendrick just explained that "I'm not the next pop star, I'm not the next socially aware rapper." But he chucks that on "HiiiPower" in the very first lines: "Visions of Martin Luther staring at me/Malcolm X put a hex on my future, someone catch me." As the last track of the album, it closes *Section.80* with mentions of revolutionary heroes like Huey Newton, Bobby Seale, Marcus Garvey, and Fred Hampton. For listeners whose first taste of Kendrick is *Section.80*, "HiiiPower" helps establish him as a Compton-born Common or Talib Kweli, a modern-day Paris[3] or (of course) Tupac. He ends the song with a shout-out to the late legend's Thug Life[4] code.

For years afterward, fans at Kendrick concerts threw three fingers in the air to symbolize the points of the "W" in "HiiiPower" during performances of the song. If "Keisha's Song (Her Pain)" and "Tammy's Song (Her Evils)" call back to feminist-leaning Tupac anthems like "Keep Ya Head Up," then HiiiPower as a concept is Kendrick's blatant take on Thug Life. Black Hippy MCs Jay Rock, Ab-Soul, and ScHoolboy Q all give HiiiPower shout-outs on their albums as a movement centered on black communal uplift. Inspiration for the song stems from a dream Kendrick repeatedly mentioned to media in 2011, where Tupac Shakur appears with a message: "Keep doing what you're doing; don't let my music die." Throughout his life, R&B singer D'Angelo had sleeping visions of the late Marvin Gaye—"I know you're wondering why you keep dreaming about me," he told him. Eighties' soul man Terence Trent D'Arby says he dreamed that John Lennon "basically walk[ed] into" him the night the former Beatle was murdered. It'd be cynical to say that Kendrick never dreamed of Tupac at all, that he concocted the whole story to create an association

---

[2] Busta Rhymes appeared on a remix that November.
[3] The militant San Fran rapper, known as the Black Panther of hiphop, released records like *The Devil Made Me Do It* in the 1990s.
[4] THUG Life = The Hate U Gave Lil' Infants Fucks Everyone.

with the rap god in everyone's head. But we all dream about what we obsess over, our unconscious minds sorting through repressed fixations and unresolved fascinations. The fact that Tupac Shakur was one of Kendrick Lamar's comes as no surprise.

But "HiiiPower" is how it ends. *Section.80* opens with a skit of a fireside chat from Kendrick, his voice pitched way down low. Posing as a cultural nationalist elder, he stands on the neighborhood corner as a campfire crackles, promising conversation "about a lot of shit that concerns you." He beckons Tammy and Keisha to come up front, characters who appear later on the album and even on its follow-up. (In 2012, "Sing About Me, I'm Dying of Thirst" will feature Kendrick rhyming from the perspective of Keisha's sister on *good kid, m.A.A.d city*.) "Fuck Your Ethnicity" properly launches the album. With a post-racial chorus ("I don't give a fuck if you black, white, Asian, Hispanic, goddammit/That don't mean shit to me") and references to both hiphop's politically conscious era and the civil rights movement ("Reporting live from Planet Terminator X[5]/I saw Martin Luther King with an AK-47"), Kendrick sets the stage for politics.

---

[5] Terminator X is the ostrich-farming former DJ of Public Enemy.

*"[Section.8o] was definitely the first time he came on my radar. I think that one is like one of those albums I look at as the first glimpse of a golden age. I'd say that's* Music of My Mind, *and* Overly Dedicated *is like* Where I'm Coming From— *where you're first hearing, OK, he's got something.* Section.8o, *that's a full-on concept album, and he's got the chops—on a song-by-song basis—to be giving you bangers within that project and then have this grand vision that he's bringing together. You could hear that this is the type of ambitious artist who's gonna aim high, and they have the discipline and ability to collaborate that can make it come to fruition.* To Pimp a Butterfly *is where you really see that ability to collaborate. But* Section.8o, *that's the first glimpse of, ahhh, OK, it's gonna be that* type *of artist."*

—JAY SMOOTH

What does he do with the moment? Not all that much, politically speaking. Couched in wordplay super elevated from his K-Dot days, essential takeaways include appreciation for the diversity of his audience, a thumbs-down to racism, the introduction of HiiiPower, and an ironic quick quip that "I'm no activist." Rejecting the activism of rappers like dead prez while dropping knowledge in his rhymes anyway throws a light on the conflict Kendrick must have felt assuming that kind of role. With idols like N.W.A and Snoop spinning ghetto narratives about life in hard-core L.A., Kendrick made clear in his discography up until this point that he fully intended to do the same. *The Kendrick Lamar EP*, *Overly Dedicated*, and, now, *Section.8o* make plain that his signature as an MC is weaving autobiography, spirituality, street politics, and gangsterism into something hiphop hasn't seen since Tupac Shakur. But to avoid being pigeonholed into the lane of conscious backpack rappers, Kendrick keeps throwing listeners off the scent. So amidst rhymes about racism still being alive and being down with God, he felt the need to assert that he wasn't an activist. And to be fair, he wasn't. But that never meant he didn't share their concerns.

With an artfully arranged still life, the cover of *Section.8o* reveals what we're in for in the music. A stack of books in the corner of a desk include Elias Aboujaoude's *Virtually You: The*

*Dangerous Powers of the E-Personality* and Robert Greene's *The Art of Seduction* topped with the Holy Bible. Resting on the Bible: a joint and a lighter. We see cash, a condom box, medicinal marijuana in a container next to a weed pipe. As well as bullets and a gun clip, a tube of lipstick and a gold-link watch band, all atop what looks like a CD sleeve for the album we're about to hear. Tracks entitled "Kush & Corinthians (His Pain)," "No Makeup (Her Vice)," and "Blow My High (Members Only)" come as no surprise then. Explaining the cover onstage at an Apple Store interview in October 2012, Kendrick told AllHipHop founder Chuck Creekmur:

> **It's taboos of the world . . . My whole thing about the gun clip and the condoms next to the Bible is, people think if you have a Bible, there's supposed to be some holy water next to it. That's a person that's already saved. I'm not speaking on them; they're good. I'm speaking on a person that's looking at this clip he just put on the drawer, these condoms, a woman's lipstick and this Bible. It's showing that he's a human being, but he's trying to find himself at the same time.**

Jay-Z served the world *Reasonable Doubt* on his own indie label, Roc-a-Fella Records, in '96. His debut gives us the fully formed Jay-Z we all know, not some beta version finding his way. *Section.80* isn't as good, but the Kendrick Lamar we get here is equally 100 percent Kendrick Lamar. In future interviews, he admits that his concept for *good kid, m.A.A.d city* already existed for years. *Section.80*'s introduction of Keisha, then, is a calculated move. The seventeen-year-old star of "Keisha's Song (Her Pain)," a rape victim of her mother's boyfriend at the age of nine, hustles as a sex worker on Long Beach Boulevard. We meet her earlier on the album; she covers a black eye with heavy foundation on "No Makeup (Her Vice)." Kendrick invokes Tupac's "Brenda's Got a Baby," Shakur's testament to another young, black, murdered sex worker; Keisha listens to the song while a pervert yells at her. Kendrick means well, forefronting the anxieties of a sexually abused call girl. But did she have to die in the end, "left for dead, raped in the street" after getting stabbed? Did Pac have to kill Brenda too? Their choices remind me of the *Sex and the City* writers' room afflicting the sexually liberated Samantha Jones with breast cancer, backhanded misogyny lurking underneath the feminism.

A month after *Section.80* hit the internet, Kendrick wept onstage. The next rung up the ladder of his pop culture climb came at The Music Box in L.A. On the verge of releasing his fourth album[6] days later, Game rushed the stage, kicking a freestyle and gamboling around like Kendrick's big brother. "It comes a time in a nigga's career, after what's gon' be four platinum albums Tuesday, when you gotta pass the motherfuckin' torch," he said. Suddenly Kurupt and Snoop appeared, blazing a fat blunt in full view of drug-averse security. "You got the torch, nigga, you better run with that motherfucker," Snoop announced, the pause in the show punctuated with air horns. Dr. Dre sat smiling in a VIP room upstairs. August 19, 2011 marked a changing of the guard in West Coast hiphop with worldwide repercussions, Kendrick's tears baptizing the recorded moment all over again with every YouTube click.

*Good kid, m.A.A.d city* was where I hopped on, and I was hardly an outlier. Over two and a half million more people bought *good kid, m.A.A.d city* than *Section.80*. The album debuted on the *Billboard* chart at number two; *Section.80* never cracked the top hundred.

On October 22, 2012, I was celebrating my son's fifth birthday when *good kid, m.A.A.d city* hit iTunes and brick-and-mortar record stores. My first week as the digital arts and culture editor at *Ebony* magazine had just wrapped up. And I'd been back in the United States for sixteen months. When I'd left for France eight years back, publishing a book of essays I originally wanted to call *The Death of Hiphop*, I felt like the hiphop world as I understood it no longer existed. Lyrics and originality didn't seem to matter as much, record sales meant far too much, MCs had no reverence for rap's roots, etc. (Nas later made the same complaints on his eighth album, *Hiphop Is Dead*.) In retrospect, things were just evolving without me at the ripe old age of thirty-three. I jetted away from my country and hiphop culture at the same time,

---

[6] That album is *The R.E.D. Album*. Kendrick makes a guest appearance on "The City."

144

only perking up my ears for Kanye West and the occasional Jay-Z and Nicki Minaj albums[7]. I was a hiphop expatriate and I grew up, a married dad living on the other side of the world. Now I was back.

Hurricane Sandy started whipping furious winds up the East Coast, my kid was in Harlem singing "Bon Anniversaire" and blowing out candles on a Superman cake, *good kid, m.A.A.d city* dropped, and it was my responsibility (once again) to be current with such things. So I listened.

Kendrick's first studio album on a major label, executive produced by Dr. Dre, opens with a prayer. Using a *Pulp Fiction*–inspired chronological order, the prayer appears again much later. As an opener, it's toned down from the bombastic intros of classics like Snoop Dogg's *Doggystyle* or Biggie's *Ready to Die*, but it's just as effective. While we're talking classics, Kendrick comes with a concept album as boldfaced as *De La Soul Is Dead* or Kanye's sorrowful *808s & Heartbreak*; it's a movie for the ears. Seventeen-year-old Kendrick rolls through Compton with his crew, tempted by the feminine wiles of Sherane[8]. Two guys in black hoodies jump Kendrick when he arrives at her house. Out for revenge, he smokes weed for courage, but the joint is laced with angel dust (PCP/phencyclidine). Then random gang-bangers murder Dave, a homie in his posse; Dave's brother gets killed in his retaliation attempt. Finally, Kendrick recites the Sinner's Prayer with someone's evangelizing grandma in a Food 4 Less parking lot and gets spiritually saved. With encouragement from his mom, Kendrick throws himself into his music and emerges on top, rapping through a victory lap duet with Dr. Dre, the album-closing "Compton." The end.

The album cover reads *good kid, m.A.A.d city: A Short Film by Kendrick Lamar*, and the record clearly earns the subtitle. Kendrick's parents recorded answering-machine skits for the album—Mom demanding her van back, Dad stressed over his dominoes —that lend Kendrick the same sense of being protected by family that saved Tre Styles from gang life in *Boyz n the Hood*. The hand of Top Dawg Entertainment is so firm that the Dre collaboration registers as one of the weakest songs on the album.

---

[7] From 2004 to 2011, I also cocked an ear toward Lupe Fiasco, Game, Drake, Raekwon, Rick Ross, Wu-Tang Clan and 50 Cent. But most were one-time spins.

[8] Sherane existed five projects ago. K-Dot rhymes on "Preach," from his 2008 mixtape, *No Sleep Til NYC*: "Champagne no, sweet Kool-Aid made by Sherane/ Send her back to her boyfriend with cum stains."

(Dre doesn't directly produce anything on *good kid, m.A.A.d city.*) Kendrick keeps guests to a minimum, but Snoop and Dre appear, as well as '90s Compton legend MC Eiht, TDE's Jay Rock, and rap's leader of the new school, Drake.

Technically, Kendrick Lamar's first album could be considered 2003's *Y.H.N.I.C. (Hub City Threat: Minor of the Year)* mixtape. *Section.80* holds a much stronger claim to the title. But *good kid, m.A.A.d city* counts as his debut to the widest, most popular audience that Kendrick had ever appeared before up until that point. This was the platform of Tupac, Eminem, and all the other rap gods he'd idolized since middle school. Soon the fifty-sixth annual Grammy Awards nominated *good kid, m.A.A.d city* for Album of the Year next to Taylor Swift and Daft Punk, along with four other nominations. He lost them all but became an immediate Grammy darling nevertheless, a household name to over twenty-eight million viewers watching the telecast in January 2014. For the first time, his songs dominated radio: "Swimming Pools (Drank)" (a gold-selling, top twenty pop hit); "Poetic Justice" (another gold, top thirty pop hit); "Bitch, Don't Kill My Vibe" peaked in the pop top forty with a remix featuring Jay-Z, the ultimate mama-I-made-it moment. Kendrick Lamar was now officially The Man.

Over at *Ebony*, hardly a bastion of up-and-coming MCs, we started debating a Kendrick Lamar cover.

"Kendrick Lamar is that new fuel," Rakim told Montreality after the 2015 release of *To Pimp a Butterfly*. "It's a conscious new fuel where he's not just doing what's hot for today. He has substance, and he ain't scared to make a statement either. And he's nice, man." That year Chuck D revealed to *Maxim* magazine that the next Public Enemy album—*Man Plans, God Laughs*—was inspired by Kendrick. Run-DMC's DMC said on a podcast: "Yo, he is hiphop. He's doing hiphop the right way. He has a truth of our existence that the young guy can relate to, that I can relate to now, that's missing in hiphop."

No pressure, then. Even as millions of Grammy watchers learned his name for the first time in the sphere of pop music, Rakim, Chuck D, DMC and a thousand other MCs old and new put *good kid, m.A.A.d city* into heavy rotation. Overwhelming respect for Kendrick came from all corners. Consider this timeline. 1) April 2011:

Kendrick shares the coveted freshman class cover of *XXL* magazine with Meek Mill, Diggy Simmons, YG, Mac Miller, and six other MCs who have yet to break out of the underground. 2) August 2012: Kendrick shares the cover of *XXL* again, this time with Dr. Dre looming behind him. #cosign. 3) October 2012: *good kid, m.A.A.d city* debuts at the top of *Billboard*'s pop chart, right behind Taylor Swift's *Red*. 4) August 2013: Kendrick appears on Big Sean's "Control," dissing eleven different MCs, Big Sean included. The verse and its hiphop aftershock become instantly legendary. 5) October 2013: Kendrick opens the *Yeezus* tour of Kanye West, the first of seven dates. The album represents Ye's creative peak, and Kendrick's arena exposure on the national tour is monumental. 6) January 2014: Kendrick performs "m.A.A.d city" at the Grammy Awards with rock band Imagine Dragons, his first major-label record up for Album of the Year. 7) March 2015: TDE/Aftermath release Kendrick's second major label LP, *To Pimp a Butterfly*.

As should be clear by now, Kendrick hardly owes his whole career to Dr. Dre. The good doctor didn't produce anything on *good kid, m.A.A.d city* or any of his future albums. And though Dre's stamp of approval eventually landed Snoop and 50 Cent into the realm of Martha Stewart and Starz network TV shows, there are a slew of Dre-endorsed rappers who suffered horrendous failures to launch. Forgive yourself for never having heard of Knoc-Turn'al, Bishop Lamont, Stat Quo, Slim the Mobster, Dawaun Parker, Hittman, or The Last Emperor. Outside of hiphop historians, no one has. Talent and preparation don't always equal up to presented opportunity. Dre signed all seven MCs, but only Google can explain why none of them became an Eminem or a Kendrick Lamar. Dr. Dre's imprimatur doesn't always guarantee wild success, or any success.

By springtime 2015, plans for my *Ebony* magazine cover story solidified. TDE president, Dave Free, and new editor-in-chief, Kierna Mayo, set up an April photo shoot and interview date out in California. *To Pimp a Butterfly* appealed to my love for jazz, concept albums, and left-of-field artistic statements all at once. I loved the new record so much that I took time out from editing to review it myself:

# Kendrick Lamar Voices the Ferguson Era

## Review by Miles Marshall Lewis

We can finally take *Black Messiah* off repeat; masterpiece two has arrived. *To Pimp a Butterfly*, Kendrick Lamar's thematically and musically layered sixteen-track sophomore album, amazes for any number of reasons. For one, the twenty-seven-year-old MC said he'd been listening to plenty of Miles Davis and Parliament while recording, and though those influences might've raised cynical eyebrows, jazz inflections and funk haven't sounded so good on a hiphop album in forever. For another, this record is easily equal if not superior to 2012's *good kid, m.A.A.d city*, which means Kendrick's done what even his idol Snoop Dogg failed to do—besting his own major label debut. (In over two decades, did Snoop ever top *Doggystyle*?)

"For Free? (Interlude)" could be a comic outtake from Max Roach's *We Insist!* or some 1970s Gil Scott-Heron album. After some initial cliché hoodrat ranting ("I need that Brazilian wavy twenty-eight-inch") over sax and jazz pianist Robert Glasper's kinetic keys, Kendrick comes in with "this dick ain't freeee" and starts scat emceeing for sixty seconds of hilarity. But the modulations of his voice and the intricacies of his rhyme—over *jazz!!*—are pure bananas, elevating "For Free?" way above the throwaway it could've been.

On the jazz side, Lalah Hathaway guests on "Complexion (A Zulu Love)," where Kendrick and 9th Wonder protégé Rapsody rhapsodize about skin tone (ironic, given the controversy over K-Dot's *Rolling Stone* cover with a possibly/probably white woman braiding his hair). Father of funk George Clinton helps open the entire album on the opener, "Wesley's Theory" (which, it should be noted, begins with the sound of needle on vinyl, not unlike the virtual side two of D'Angelo's recent *Black Messiah*).

The jazz-soul-funk bona fides don't stop there: Bilal sings on "Institutionalized," Ron Isley appears on "How Much a Dollar Cost." Quietly, producer Flying Lotus is the cousin of Ravi Coltrane, the grand-nephew of Alice Coltrane. Snoop shows up too (on "Institutionalized"), as does Pharrell (singing the hook to "Alright"), Pete Rock (scratching on "Complexion [A Zulu Love]") and Dr. Dre

(via voicemail on "Wesley's Theory"). The eclectic musical bed and pedigree of *To Pimp a Butterfly* suits the lyrical content, which is an equally beautiful mess of ideas ranging from self-loathing ("u") to self-love (the Grammy-winning "i"), black power ("The Blacker the Berry") to sex ("These Walls") to spirituality ("Momma").

The concept album can be dangerous territory when what you're shooting for outweighs what you can actually pull off, but in a repeat of *good kid, m.A.A.d city*, K. Dot manages to do it again. The record is laced with a recurring poem ("I remember you was conflicted, misusing your influence," "Resentment... turned into a deep depression") that finally unfurls in full at the closer, "Mortal Man." At that point, having pretty much just concluded the best hiphop album since *My Beautiful Dark Twisted Fantasy*, dear listeners learn he's been sharing the poem all along in an imaginary dialogue with (SPOILER ALERT, but you'll really wanna know this) Tupac Shakur. Who answers back (!) in a five-minute conversation, courtesy of cutting and splicing from a 1994 interview with Swedish journalist Mats Nileskär.

Of course there are hiphop quotables: "Critics want to mention that they miss when hiphop was rappin'/Motherfucker, if you did, then Killer Mike would be platinum"; "How many leaders you said you needed then left 'em for dead?" "Life ain't shit but a fat vagina." Cast as the central character of *Roots* on the '70s funk-styled "King Kunta," Kendrick makes direct allusions to James Brown's classic "The Payback" with his "I could dig rapping" and "I'm mad," complete with female background voices egging him on.

With the voice of an embattled black man, K-Dot embodies the zone of African-American youth in the Ferguson era all over *To Pimp a Butterfly*. If it's an instant classic, it's because it's entirely of the moment. If excellence comes in threes, my money says Frank Ocean got next.

Like I mentioned, *Rolling Stone* awarded Kendrick the cover that same week. (The "possibly/ probably white woman" twisting his hair was actually his light-skinned fiancée and the mother of his young daughter, Whitney Alford.) In the internet era, *Rolling Stone* doesn't hold the same cachet as it used to, but as a bible of pop culture since the late 1960s, singers once wrote songs about getting the cover. In 2013 *GQ*, a Condé Nast publication with much of the same track record regarding rap artists, also awarded him the cover —whipping a microphone cord at the camera in a tailored Emporio Armani suit, skinny tie, and suspenders. But for years, no one else from *XXL*'s annual freshman issues ever graduated to the cover of *Rolling Stone*[9]. No other MCs from Black Hippy have received the cover, nor will they. *Rolling Stone* is for the hallowed heights of Run-DMC and MC Hammer, of Jay-Z, Lauryn Hill, OutKast, Dre and Snoop, the Fugees, Eminem, Kanye, Tupac, Diddy, and Lil Wayne. Since Kendrick, the magazine has anointed Migos, Cardi B, Megan Thee Stallion and Lil Baby too. A total of nineteen rap acts for a biweekly magazine over fifty years old. Kendrick Lamar scoring the cover of *Rolling Stone*—twice at this point—means a certain thing.

"*The other thing about* DAMN. *is that it could almost be like a long-form work. When I play* DAMN., *I do it like I do* The Miseducation of Lauryn Hill. *Like, I kinda wanna hear all of 'em! I think we were all just blown away by his innovativeness and creativity. Everybody on that [Pulitzer] committee is a music lover in our different genres. We were just like: Every form produces its best, right? It would be better to just have the best of all those forms kind of sitting against each other rather than saying, 'These are the only genres we're going to listen to.' And Kendrick definitely held his own there.*"

—FARAH JASMINE GRIFFIN

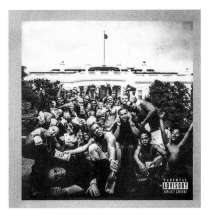

---

[9] *XXL* freshman class alum Megan Thee Stallion graced the cover of *Rolling Stone* in 2020, following Travis Scott in 2018, and Future in 2016.

Repeated listening peels back even more layers of *To Pimp a Butterfly*. Achieving ultimate mainstream success with *good kid, m.A.A.d city* gave Kendrick a serious case of survivor's guilt; he says exactly that in his recurring poem written to Tupac. Kendrick lays out his poem in full at the end of "Mortal Man," addressing mental health in a way rarely heard from rappers, black male pop stars, or black men in general. Following his spoken word, Kendrick feels conflicted about misusing and abusing the power of his newfound influence. He felt (in the recent past) full of self-loathing from rising above his circumstances in Compton while his homies stayed behind, which snowballed into a deep depression. Surrounded by the temptations of fame and success, Kendrick went searching for answers in Africa—February 2014 concert dates in South Africa (Johannesburg, Cape Town, and Durban) inspired the entire album—only to return to America with survivor's guilt. Chad Keaton, the younger brother of a close friend currently locked up in prison, died on August 14, 2013, from a drive-by shooting while Kendrick was on tour somewhere between Sweden and Belgium. Guilt set in over not somehow saving Chad's life or being there at the hospital as he suffered from gunshot wounds, guilt he expresses on "u." ("A friend never leave Compton for profit/Or leave his best friend little brother/You promised you'd watch him before they shot him," he rhymes. Elsewhere, he blames himself for not preventing the pregnancy of his little sister, Kayla Duckworth, in 2014, when she was thirteen years old.) Kendrick concludes the poem explaining that his world travels gave him an appreciation for black solidarity and unification, a lesson he feels responsible to share with his crew in Compton. The overarching themes of *To Pimp a Butterfly*—fame, exploitation, black pride, survivor's guilt, depression—all expand outward from his poem to Tupac, apropos for an album originally titled *Tu Pimp a Caterpillar* (acronym: TuPaC).

In May 2015, top-forty radio started spinning the fourth single from Taylor Swift's pop masterwork, *1989*: "Bad Blood," featuring verses from Kendrick Lamar. For most of the African-American community, the twentysomething pop princess exists mainly as a culture-vulture punch line. Kanye West famously interrupted her acceptance speech at the 2009 MTV Video Awards when her largely forgotten visual for "You Belong With Me" won out over Beyoncé's more innovative "Single Ladies

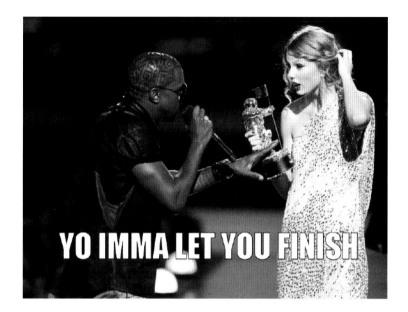

(Put a Ring On It)" clip. Their coupling extended to 2016, when Ye mentioned her on "Famous" as a bitch he made famous, one whom he still might have sex with. (She denied giving him permission for the dis, only for Kim Kardashian West to later Snapchat audio of Swift's approval.) In other quarters, Quincy Jones screwed up his face in a *GQ* interview when asked about her: "We need more songs, man. Fucking songs, not hooks." Comedy dynamic duo Desus and Mero appeared on *The Tonight Show* and brought host Jimmy Fallon to tears by mentioning her "really long back"—meaning her flat behind, the traditional white girl insult. And Black Twitter tore apart her 2019 *Billboard* Music Awards performance for blatantly ripping off the iconic Coachella set Beyoncé immortalized in Netflix's *Homecoming*.

Taylor Swift is not black America's favorite celebrity. Kendrick Lamar still leveraged her ask into his first appearance on a number-one pop hit. My youngest son, who turned five the day *good kid, m.A.A.d city* came out, loved her back then. As with scores of other tweeners and elementary school kids, "Bad Blood" became the first time my second grader ever heard of Kendrick Lamar. (I blame myself.)

"*To Pimp a Butterfly is the album that I take when my jazz-head friends are like, 'This hiphop stuff [sucks].' I'm like, 'You need to listen to To Pimp a Butterfly.' There are those albums in our tradition that are like, the whole tradition is up in there. You can hear it. I don't wanna hear you all talking about how this is not engaging jazz. Are you kidding me? I think that's what probably made me listen*"
—FARAH JASMINE GRIFFIN

The Recording Academy awarded *To Pimp a Butterfly* a total of eleven Grammy nominations, more than any previous rapper ever, one shy of the record set with Michael Jackson's *Thriller*. His inventive, introspective career milestone lost to *1989* for Album for the Year. Kendrick swept every single rap category—Best Rap Album, Best Rap Song ("Alright"), Best Rap Performance ("Alright") and Best Rap/Sung Collaboration ("These Walls")—as well as Music Video, for "Bad Blood." For the first time, his accomplishments weren't mirrored by past achievements from Jay-Z, Kanye West, Eminem, or most of the other MCs he once looked to for direction and inspiration. Kendrick Lamar had become uniquely his own phenomenon.

According to a 2017 Nielsen Music report, R&B/hiphop finally became the biggest, most listened to music genre in the United States. But going pop destroyed the careers of many an MC at the very beginning of MCs going pop. That particular graveyard teems with the likes of one- or two-hit wonders like Vanilla Ice, Young MC, Gerardo, and Tone Lōc. The beauty of hiphop transforming America to become its pop music is that the culture did so on its own terms, bending people's tastes to its own flavor rather than diluting itself in the way that those six-feet-under MCs once did. N.W.A topped the *Billboard* chart with its own authenticity intact, without, say, collaborating with a rock band like Aerosmith to get over. Rap was never the same.

That's not to say that getting in bed with pop music can't ultimately lose you your original audience. Most rap lovers in my circle prefer early mixtape Nicki Minaj far more than the Nicki Minaj of 6ix9ine's "Trollz." The Taylor Swift–collaborating Kendrick Lamar could have fallen prey to oversaturation. But either TDE proved way too savvy for that or he got lucky. Up until his complete pop coronation at the 2016 Grammys, Kendrick appeared on a series of songs that could've given the impression that he'd sold out but somehow didn't. The L.A. indie rock band Awolnation tapped Kendrick and Ab-Soul for a remix to their "Sail" single way back in 2011. He shows up with equal energy for the electropop queen Dido ("Let Us Move On," 2012); *Saturday Night Live* jokesters Lonely Island ("YOLO," 2013); Robin Thicke's follow-up to his "Blurred Lines" smash ("Give It 2 U," 2013); and Grammy collaborators Imagine Dragons ("Radioactive," 2014). Kendrick planted seeds way outside of hiphop for years, another something that Dr. Dre's anointing made possible.

Kendrick Lamar cultivated a reputation as a throwback to the far-gone days of lyricism and social relevancy as the uppermost values in hiphop. Mumble rap has its place. Emo rap as well. But for anyone appreciating rap music for the lyrical standards upheld today by Run the Jewels

*"Everyone's gonna have their different definitions of a classic. But I think [good kid, m.A.A.d city] had a huge impact, made a big dent commercially, connoisseurs and critics love it. I think it's really influential for where the scene was headed. It's one of those records that's one of the biggest hits that is also at the avant-garde. It's a benchmark too for how the music is developing in general, how his art is evolving. I don't see any standard where you wouldn't say it's a classic."*
—JAY SMOOTH

**153**

*"Because the Pulitzers are every year, and the nominees have to be things that have come out that year, there was a big conversation about, 'Well, is this the greatest hiphop? What about Biggie? And what about Nas?' But then we were like, 'You know what? That's not what's here right now. So, of this year, what is it about this?' Sonically, there was a richness there, a kind of engagement that we were hearing across the board in the pieces that we nominated. There was a complexity of texture that we all found very compelling. It was a combination of, both lyrically and sonically, the kind of story that was being told. [DAMN. was] a piece of art that was very much of its time, and yet we felt could stand the test of time."*

—FARAH JASMINE GRIFFIN

or Black Thought, Kendrick Lamar sat at the top of that list as the most instantly familiar "real rapper" one could name at the drop of a dime by 2016. That standing led to several bookings on American talk shows forever looking for hip demographics. Kendrick took those opportunities to tease new material instead of continually trotting out "Alright." Post–*To Pimp a Butterfly*, the time was right for another mixtape or some other album that wasn't quite an album. Studio outtakes made perfect sense.

Kendrick appeared on *The Colbert Report* as the final musical act on comedian Stephen Colbert's canceled show in December 2014. Far later, January 2016, Kendrick performed another unknown, untitled song[10] on *The Tonight Show*, and tacked on some brand-new verses at the end of his Grammy Awards performance[11] that February. At the urging of basketball star LeBron James[12], TDE released *untitled unmastered* two months afterward. Not technically a mixtape or an official new record—it wasn't received as the New Kendrick Lamar Album—*untitled unmastered* qualified as a compilation album, a stopgap odds-and-sods collection of demos that failed to make *To Pimp a Butterfly*. Releasing *untitled unmastered* intentionally took some air out of Kendrick's

---

[10] *untitled unmastered* revealed that song to be "untitled 03 | 05.28.2013.

[11] *untitled unmastered* revealed that song to be "untitled 05 | 09.21.2014."

[12] LeBron James (@KingJames) to Top Dawg on Twitter: "Yo @dangerookipawaa after that @kendricklamar Grammy performance, you have to release those untitled tracks asap!! What's up? Talk to me."

balloon before it popped (no pun intended). Meanwhile, in the space where he'd become instantly familiar, Beyoncé blessed him with one of the most coveted guest appearances in pop music on "Freedom." Their modern ode to black liberation put community first at a point in their careers when crossover artists from the past were getting rhinoplasty and taking other measures to soften their blackness for a wider white audience. The difference in approach speaks to the authenticity mainstream audiences want from African-American artists nowadays, and the noncompromise that black artists approach their own careers with in the post-hiphop era.

True story: I asked the millennial students of my NYU class "Who is U2 to you?" and someone raised her hand to say that they're the rock group who stuck an album they didn't want onto their smartphones. Because it's true, Apple did upload *Songs of Innocence* onto every iPhone overnight through an exclusive deal in 2014. And U2's last top forty hit in America goes back to 2004, when most kids in my class were in kindergarten. U2 mean an entirely different thing to me, as might be expected.

U2, for me, is all tied up in the teenage girl whose parents left my Bronx hood for the suburbs. "They care so much for their fans," she said, over the push-button phone of her dad's man cave on Long Island. Bono, the Edge,

*"To Pimp a Butterfly is this big prestige album that [would attract] people who want to be culturally aware. I'm gonna see in People magazine this is an album I'm supposed to know. Then people see his name and they're gonna check for it."*
—JAY SMOOTH

**155**

Adam Clayton, and Larry Mullen Jr. ruled her new majority-white high school with socially conscious songs like the Martin Luther King, Jr. tribute "Pride (In the Name of Love)." I didn't listen right away. When *The Joshua Tree* beat Prince's *Sign o' the Times* for Album of the Year at the Grammys, I called bullshit. But then a funny thing happened. My public high school choir sang onstage with U2 at Madison Square Garden, for a gospel version of "I Still Haven't Found What I'm Looking For." I lined up for the *Rattle and Hum* concert movie to see my classmates and walked out a fan, posters of U2 and Sheila E. taped to the walls of my college dorm room. Even so, *Pop* was the last U2 album I played more than once, over twenty years back. Lead singer Bono transitioned into a humanitarian elder statesman long ago, more famous for his Bono Talk (words of wisdom he doles out to the newly famous) than U2's latest album. If my college students didn't grow up on U2, certainly Kendrick didn't. But the limited lineup of guest features on 2017's *DAMN.*, his first real studio album since *To Pimp a Butterfly*, included Rihanna, DJ Kid Capri, and U2.

Sometime in late 2016, Bono asked Kendrick to appear on the group's fourteenth studio album, *Songs of Experience*. "It was really just that we were fans," U2 guitarist the Edge told Stereogum. "We were just thinking about artists we really respect and like, and he was on the top of our list," Bono agreed. "There's a righteous anger that is hard to argue with," he added. "I asked him would he rap about where America is at. His reply was to rap about where America isn't at. Smart dude." Kendrick shows up twice on *Songs of Experience*: the album single "Get Out of Your Own Way" and "American Soul." But while U2 returned to the drawing board to tweak their album before release, Kendrick asked permission to use Bono's recurring verse on "American Soul" for his own album. *DAMN.*'s "XXX." deals with the systemic effect of white supremacy on everyday black American lives, and the country's moral hypocrisy.

The Pulitzer Prize board unanimously awarded *DAMN.* the Pulitzer Prize for Music on April 16, 2018. *DAMN.* scored five Grammy nominations, including (again) Album of the Year. And Kendrick lost out on their highest honor (again), this time to Bruno Mars. But a Pulitzer Prize for Music has never been awarded to a pop or hiphop album since its inception in 1943. Stevie Wonder's *Songs in the Key of Life* doesn't have one. Nor does Marvin Gaye's *What's Going On*, nor Miles Davis's

*Kind of Blue*. The board passed over Duke Ellington in 1965 and didn't award a prize to a jazz album until 1997, to Wynton Marsalis's *Blood on the Fields*. In 2018, the Pulitzer nominating committee pored over so many hiphop-influenced works that someone suggested they pay attention to an actual hiphop recording, Kendrick Lamar's *DAMN*. On May 30, 2018, he accepted his Pulitzer in a ceremony at Columbia University in New York City. The Pulitzer board's announcement called *DAMN*. "a virtuosic song collection, unified by its vernacular authenticity and rhythmic dynamism that offers affecting vignettes capturing the complexity of modern African-American life."

Around the time of Kendrick's win, think pieces sprouted everywhere debating whether or not the gatekeepers of these elite awards had loosened the locks and chains a bit. "Bob Dylan Wins Nobel Prize, Redefining Boundaries of Literature" read a *New York Times* headline in late 2016, when the Nobel Committee gifted the folk singer with the same Nobel Prize in Literature presented in the past to Toni Morrison and Gabriel García Márquez. As the first musician to receive the award, his win sparked debate about song lyrics holding the same artistic value as a novel or poetry. No one gets lionized as the voice of his generation more than Bob Dylan. Though he's been recording music decades longer than Kendrick, the literary value of their material is equal. Dylan's "Outlaw Blues" is no more or less painstakingly descriptive than Kendrick's "The Art of Peer Pressure" when he paints a picture of "Me and my niggas four deep in a white Toyota/A quarter tank of gas, one pistol, and orange soda." The recognition of both storytellers was bound to cause controversy, but the ruffled feathers didn't make either of them any less deserving.

For its themes and musical innovation, *To Pimp a Butterfly* is just as worthy of the Pulitzer Prize for Music, maybe even more so, as *DAMN*. The whole consideration behind which works of music were also suitable for appreciation returns us to the world of Earth-Two fantasy. If *DAMN*. was a Pulitzer-warranted hiphop album, then—artistically, thematically, sonically—so are Nas's *Illmatic*, De La Soul's *Buhloone Mindstate* and *The Miseducation of Lauryn Hill*. And so on, down the slippery slope of Kanye's *My Beautiful Dark Twisted Fantasy*, Dilla's *Donuts*, Jay-Z's *4:44*, etc. Honored

for "her indelible contribution to American music and culture for more than five decades," Aretha Franklin received a posthumous Special Citation from the Pulitzer Prize board the year after *DAMN.*'s win. But Dylan, Ellington, John Coltrane, Thelonious Monk, and others won in the past; it didn't necessarily continue a pop-recognizing trend set by Kendrick. The 2019 Pulitzer Prize for Music went to Ellen Reid's *p r i s m*, an opera confronting the effects of sexual and emotional abuse, and 2020 awarded another opera, Anthony Davis's *The Central Park Five*. But Kendrick Lamar's victory stands as a revolutionary moment for hip-hop, and for pop music as well. His journey from being a teenage dreamer in Compton setting intentions to becoming a Pulitzer-winning pop artist sounds just like an Earth Two imaginary story. But Kendrick really managed to manifest it all. And he hasn't even reached his twilight zone.

# Chapter 5

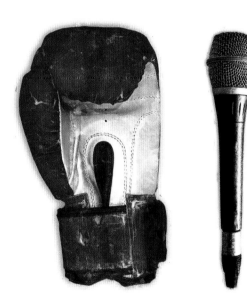

# The Spiteful Chant

## 1.

The Beatles masterminded the most famous album cover of all time with *Sgt. Pepper's Lonely Hearts Club Band*, an album I was already tired of hearing about when I was in high school, despite never even listening to the so-called Greatest Album of All Time. Explaining the record sleeve feels like bothering to describe Egyptian pyramids or the Sphinx—like, surely you've seen it. The Fab Four sport colorful military uniforms as they stand in front of a flower arrangement honoring the burial of themselves. Roses on their grave spell out a huge BEATLES. They're surrounded by photos of over seventy famous figures pasted to huge cardboard cut-outs: Einstein, Gandhi, Laurel and Hardy, even Ab-Soul's guru Aleister Crowley. When I broke down and bought the compact disc in college, one of the things I loved most about the cover was a ragdoll placed nonchalantly next to Marilyn Monroe's high heels. The doll's shirt reads WELCOME THE ROLLING STONES in full caps.

The Beatles and the Rolling Stones—one of the most classic Apollonian-Dionysian rivalries in music history. John, Paul, George, and Ringo couldn't have known their 1967 classic would go down the way it did. But something about that Shirley Temple doll wearing a Rolling Stones sweatshirt always seemed like a poke in the ribs to me, a way for one group to tease the other about making the superior music somehow. As if the Beatles knew they were so much more incredibly important that free publicity for rivals couldn't possibly affect their status as the more untouchable force. Under the same idea, a writer frenemy released his first book when I released mine in 2004 and I almost bought his promo T-shirt to sport around

*"Look at his competition, like the top tier guys. Everybody loves J. Cole, I get it. But for those of us who grew up with MCs who are also producers and also look at the guys on the underground—like Black Milk, Oddisee, or Roc Marciano—we could name about fifteen guys who we like way better and make way better material. J. Cole has the backing and the name. He came up in the mixtape thing, and he has the corporate backing so that he's the guy out there. But we don't listen to J. Cole like that. I've heard better shit from Oddisee. But that's neither here nor there. The point I'm making is that Kendrick is head and shoulders above all the top tier guys."*
—DART ADAMS

Brooklyn. (I didn't think anyone would get the joke though . . . ah, youth.)

*Mona Lisa* painter Leonardo da Vinci and Michelangelo, the younger artist responsible for the Sistine Chapel ceiling, had an intense dislike for each other around the turn of the sixteenth century. Exactly why has been lost to time. Jump forward three thousand years: traditional conservative Brahms and the more radically progressive Wagner belonged to a war of the Romantics in classical music, the two composers really not feeling each other either. Cubism—considered the most influential art movement of modern times—came into vogue when master painters Pablo Picasso and Georges Braque forged their own frenemy relationship to create the style. They painted side by side in southern France in the summer of 1911 and bystanders could hardly tell their works apart, though Picasso ended up with the far more famous reputation. Intense artistic rivalries go back even earlier than the 1500s of Michelangelo; competition and jealousy are hardwired into the arts, into human nature period.

Growing up on hiphop, I loved discovering that dis records existed even before rap music. After the breakup of the Beatles, John Lennon asked Paul McCartney "How Do You Sleep?" in 1971 ("The sound you make is Muzak to my ears/You must have learned something in all those years"). Back in 1960, R&B singer Joe Tex called out James Brown on "You Keep Her," based on a lover the men had in common ("James, I got your letter, it came to me today/You said I could have my baby back, but I don't want her that way"). This music came out way before what I was weaned on, the stuff of Roxanne Shanté vs. UTFO, MC Lyte vs. Antoinette, KRS-One vs. MC Shan.

God once said—sorry, wait. So, spiritualist author Neale Donald Walsch penned a series of *New York Times* bestsellers in the 1990s called *Conversations with God*, with dialogues of what the Most High supposedly told him. Somewhere in book three, God and Walsch converse about competition and what a culture created by highly evolved beings might look like. God says, "They do not compete. They realize that when one loses, everyone loses. They therefore do not create sports and games, which teach children (and perpetuate in adults) the extraordinary thought that someone 'winning' while another is 'losing' is entertainment." Sports never appealed to me at all, I was never good at any of them, and this idea always stuck with me because it seemed to explain why. Measuring the skills of Stephen Curry against LeBron James is not a conversation I'm interested in or capable of having. However. Debating over who won the battle between LL Cool J and Kool Moe Dee, Ice Cube and N.W.A, or Jay-Z and Nas feels completely different. 50 Cent winning while Ja Rule was losing? Totally entertaining to me. Hiphop is my sports.

Kendrick Lamar couldn't level up to the top of hiphop without other MCs coming for his crown, firing lyrical potshots, and challenging his place. As a culture, hiphop has always been a space where proving your worth is necessary to defend your position. I'd seen it firsthand in St. Mary's Park in the South Bronx in the late 1970s, B-boy crews dancing against one another on folded-out slabs of cardboard boxes. And later in the '80s, teenage rappers at Truman High School banging out beats on cafeteria tables and rhyming against one another for nothing more than egos and reputation. Competition is in the lifeblood of hiphop, and Kendrick couldn't become the king without a handful of microphone challengers.

"Logged into my Twitter today and got a quick reminder that time is in full flight," Drake shared from his @champagnepapi Instagram account in April 2019. "A lot of blessings to be aware and appreciative of for so many of us . . . take a quick moment to digest the progression in your life no matter how small or large. Then get back to it." Nostalgia courses through most of Drake's material, his reflections on past relationships (mostly romances) making up the bulk of albums like *Views* and *Take Care*. He'd reposted Twitter direct messages going all the way back to 2009, from model Paris Morton, basketball players Kevin Durant and Tristan Thompson, R&B singer Trey Songz, and—from June 9, 2011—a pre–*Section.80* Kendrick Lamar.

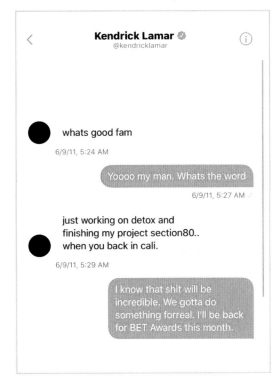

The Beatles had the Stones, Michael Jackson had Prince, Beyoncé has Rihanna, and Kendrick Lamar, for better or worse, has Drake. With a longer career, bigger streaming numbers, more Grammy nominations and a fan base arguably larger than Kendrick's, the Canadian rapper can't be left out of any serious conversation about the most popular MC in 2010s hiphop. The Coca-Cola Company resurrected its Obey Your Thirst campaign in 2015, printing lyrics from Rakim, Nas, Biggie Smalls, and Drake on Sprite soda cans—meaning the billion-dollar business picked Drake as the only representative rapper from the modern era. Rap fans sitting by Sprite's bus-stop posters in their hoods laughed to themselves; lyrically, Drake isn't considered to be anywhere near the class of those other MCs from the standpoint of the culture. Ironically though, from the perspective of mainstream popularity, none of those godlike rap artists compare to him.

Born Aubrey Drake Graham one year earlier than Kendrick up in Toronto, Ontario, classmates bullied the young Canadian over his biracial parentage (his mother was a Jewish schoolteacher, his dad an expat African-American drummer). With an affinity for the arts, Graham dropped out of high school and launched an acting career at fifteen, as the wheelchair-bound former basketball star Jimmy Brooks on the teen soap opera *Degrassi: The Next Generation*. After leaving the show, mixtapes came next—*Room for Improvement* (2006) and *Comeback Season* (2007). "Man of the Year" opened the door for his relationship with rapper Lil Wayne (Drake's song samples a Flo Rida track featuring Wayne), who invited Drake to join his North American tour and soon his Young Money Entertainment record label.

Next to the dictionary definition of guilty pleasure (something, such as a piece of music, that one enjoys despite feeling that it is not generally held in high regard), a guy wearing AirPods listens to a Drake mix. It's not that I've never moved to "Started From the Bottom" on the dance floor of some hiphop-friendly gala. But because of his penchant for narrating fragile masculinity to elicit compassion from female listeners, most of Drake's music doesn't sound made for male eavesdroppers, like the feminist hymns of Beyoncé. The first season of HBO's *Insecure*, which follows the lives of two African-American twentysomething women in L.A., features Easter eggs of Drake lyrics hidden in all its episodes. ("He just really gets us!" says lead character Issa Dee in the premiere.) Women adore him, and through all his anecdotes of unrequited love, he's pandered for their attention from the beginning of his career.

The twin poles of Drake's oeuvre involve romance and nostalgia. Hiphop isn't alien to desire at all. Drake built on the maudlin heartache of Kanye West's groundbreaking *808s & Heartbreak* to cement his style, but LL Cool J, Q-Tip, André 3000, Method Man, and others all once did their part to inject sensitivity into rap music. Drake sings nearly as much as he emcees, but even that approach harks back to the Kurtis Blow single "Daydreaming" from the ancient days of 1982. As a heartthrob MC, he upholds that lovelorn rapper tradition like no one else. The second season of the Emmy-winning surrealist comedy *Atlanta* devotes an entire episode (entitled "Champagne Papi") to on-again-off-again girlfriend Van Keefer crashing a Drake house party. He's not there; he's on tour in Europe. But she spends the episode in search of him: going through his closets, spraying his cologne, humming his songs. From *Insecure* to *Atlanta*, Drake rules the zeitgeist right now when it comes to female millennial thirst, right alongside actor Michael B. Jordan and the *Queen Sugar* heartthrob Kofi Siriboe. Rihanna may have recorded "LOYALTY." with Kendrick, complete with flirtatious video, but she actually slept with Drake.

There's no doubt babies have been conceived

*"To find an analogy to explain Kendrick's crushing dominance of 2010s hiphop, you'd have to look to game-changers like Serena Williams in tennis, LeBron James in basketball, or Steve Jobs in consumer technology. But the question of whether he would have ruled the 2010s if the playing field for MCs was as competitive as it was in the 1990s assumes that super-skilled rap icons of the 2010s like Nicki Minaj, Tierra Whack, J. Cole, Vincent Staples, Chance the Rapper, Danny Brown, and Young Thug don't matter or exist. It's way more productive to consider him as the latest and greatest in a long continuum of MCs—each of whom has raised the bar in hiphop with regard to aesthetic criteria like flow, cadence, articulation/enunciation, versatility, and timbre, not to mention issues of political and moral courage."*
—JASON KING

**169**

*"Kendrick's signature is really difficult to copy. That's because his signature is his penchant for complex multiplicity, his refusal to be reduced to any one single thing. Even some of the most gifted MCs conform to one unique flow, or they've got one timbral or rhythmic gimmick. But Kendrick effortlessly and experimentally gear-shifts between rhythms, flows, cadences, speeds, and vocal registers— sometimes all within the same song. He oscillates between punchy rapping and melodious singing, placing accents and stresses on weirdly unexpected syllables, like a hiphop version of Thelonious Monk or Cecil Taylor. He refuses to be pigeonholed into any singular sound or sonic concept, and he runs the emotional gamut, from ferocious rage to contemplative introspection. That's why his multiplicity is also a racial refusal—it's how he resists industry and cultural pressure to wind up a predictable, cliché, basic, one-dimensional stereotype."*

—JASON KING

to mood-music Drake playlists, his sound lending itself amenably to the bedroom. He also makes occasional overtures to male-dominant rap audiences—casting the sexiest women's basketball team ever in the video for "Best I Ever Had" for example, with more bouncing breasts than a Russ Meyer movie. His hiphop brings a neo-blues longing to the genre, his rhymes constantly looking back on those who doubted his rise and the unlimited ladies left in his wake. His laments have laments. To quote from the source, he's forever "running through the 6 with my woes," an extremely woe-is-me MC. Drake is also a master of the meme, with omnipresent social media gifs to prove it. He debuted his *More Life* mixtape on his own OVO Sound Radio show via Apple's Beats 1 radio station, gluing everyone to the appointment broadcast like the happy days of *American Graffiti*.

The most significant rap rivalry of the 2010s (Nicki Minaj and Cardi B aside) belongs to Kendrick Lamar and Drake. Outside of Kanye West, who lost major cultural capital by aligning himself with Donald Trump, they're the two biggest rappers on the pop landscape. As childhood witnesses to the deadly beef between Tupac Shakur and the Notorious B.I.G., both MCs tread lightly when it comes to ramping things out of control. But their relationship progressed from friendly text messages to appearing on each other's albums to a string of subliminal disses in the

**170**

wake of Kendrick's infamous 2013 verse on Big Sean's "Control." Both rappers are fully aware that a cold war trumps a war with actual casualties, which largely explains the subdued comments from each of them about the other.

Back in 2011, a week after Kendrick Lamar and Drake exchanged the texts above, Kendrick arrived in Toronto for the first time to play the Sound Academy. He'd turn twenty-four the next day. Drake was in his hometown laying down tracks at Sterling Road Studios for his second album, *Take Care*, and reached out to Kendrick. "We met up, chilled out, got to vibe, see where each other was at," Kendrick later told *XXL*. "Sometimes you like a person's music but you definitely don't like the actual artist when you sit down and you talk to them. That's a real good dude; he got a real genuine soul. We clicked immediately. We had spoken probably one time before that." Essentially, they celebrated Kendrick's birthday together. The younger MC shared a preview of his first full album, *Section.80* (released a month later), with Drake that night via email. The next month Drake invited him to appear on *Take Care*, and Kendrick's bars say a lot.

"Buried Alive (Interlude)" details the particulars of the two rap giants' first meeting in Ontario. Sandwiched between "Marvin's Room" and "Under Ground Kings," Kendrick uses his two-minute verse to speak on fame, vanity, and ego. He opens by confessing that he's embarrassed

*"Kendrick is an MC that would've fit in perfectly during the '90s. But had Kendrick been around during the '90s, he would've been competing directly with the best. I feel that Kendrick is great, without a doubt. But Kendrick is head and shoulders above his contemporaries. Largely because the mainstream rap industry is not what it used to be."*
—DART ADAMS

**171**

*"Drake is both the most commercially successful hiphop artist of the entire 2010s and the most culturally impactful male hiphop star of the Obama-era too, at least prior to* To Pimp a Butterfly. *As the first biracial, half-Jewish rapper in history to achieve mainstream success, Drake grabbed the baton from MCs like Lauryn Hill, Pharrell Williams, and Kanye West by taking 'emo hiphop' to the next level. Hiphop after Drake sounded much more melody-driven, with raw, exposed lyrics full of questioning, self-doubt, and navel-gazing introspection. His appeal is that he upended ideas about masculinity, poking fun at himself instead until he morphed into the subject of endless viral memes. Drake wasn't just one of the biggest figures in hiphop of the decade —he was easily popular music's most influential supernova altogether, next to Adele and Beyoncé."*
—JASON KING

over what he sees in the mirror post–*Section.80*; he's become a "suicidal terrorist" willing to kill the old version of himself for a mainstream reincarnation as a super-popular new Kendrick. He introduces "an alien that said last year that she slept with a Canadian," a sexy personification of the music business who's apparently already seduced Drake. Soon he's in the Palms Casino Resort of Las Vegas, choosing blowjobs over reading Bible verses, losing himself in the perks of celebrity. He ghosts his one-night stand, blaming Drake for showing him how to handle hookups as a rap star.

Then Kendrick takes it back to June 2011, cruising through Toronto in Drake's Mercedes-Maybach. "Felt like the initiation," he says, bonding with an artist who's already further along on his own meteoric rise, someone who also made noise through mixtapes and reached superstar status with help from a cosigner (Lil Wayne instead of Dr. Dre in Drake's case). They speak casually about the record industry, about female fans as the tastemakers of rap music. Kendrick turns twenty-four at the stroke of midnight. Drake won't turn twenty-five until October, so for a few months, they're the same age. Drake shares this with Kendrick—"and it didn't help 'cause it made me even more rude and impatient," he says. The atmospheric sounds and cohesive themes (past romances, the pursuit of fame, ego, and braggadocio) of Drake's acclaimed third mixtape, *So Far*

*Gone*, eclipsed the success of any of Kendrick's projects up till then. We can sense his envy and insecurity learning that Drake's career has shot higher, further, and faster in his twenty-four years. Kendrick ends "Buried Alive" explaining that we should all fault Drake for his newfound vanity and a rededicated laser focus that makes him consider leaving his best friend (Whitney Alford?) behind. "So dig a shovel full of money, full of power, full of pussy/Full of fame and bury yourself alive," he resolves. Then he dies. *Take Care* debuts at number one, selling over four million copies. *Section.80* sells five hundred thousand. As a young gun MC to watch, Kendrick does his duty with A$AP Rocky as the opening act on Drake's Club Paradise Tour—the highest grossing hiphop tour that year.

All this good will between the two led to "Poetic Justice," the fourth single off Kendrick's first mega-successful full-length album, *good kid, m.A.A.d city.* "He had asked me to get on 'Poetic Justice,'" Drake later told *XXL*. "It's a great song, but it's the typical, you know, I'm going to be on the soft girls' song on the album. So it was like, 'Let me give you some shit.'" Drake counteroffered with "Fuckin' Problems," a track that became a top ten song for A$AP Rocky (his biggest), higher on the pop chart than "Poetic Justice." Kendrick declined the song because it didn't fit his concept album's narrative. The Grammy Awards eventually pit Kendrick's magnum opus against Drake's *Nothing Was the Same* for Best Rap Album. (Both lost out to Macklemore, the least culturally impactful of the three.) But Drake and Kendrick enjoyed equal commercial success for the first time.

Then came "Control."

# 3.

On August 14, 2013—while Kendrick relaxed between music festival performances in Sweden and Belgium—Kanye West protégé Big Sean released "Control," the lead salvo from his second studio album, *Hall of Fame*. (In the end, "Control" didn't appear on *Hall of Fame*; Sean was too severely upstaged in his own song.) Kendrick called out eleven rappers by name, earning him more enemies and engendering more ill will than anything else in his entire career before or since then: "I'm usually homeboys with the same niggas I'm rhymin' with/But this is hiphop, and them niggas should know what time it is/And that goes for Jermaine Cole, Big K.R.I.T., Wale/Pusha-T, Meek Millz, A$AP Rocky, Drake/Big Sean, Jay Electron', Tyler, Mac Miller/I got love for you all, but I'm tryna murder you niggas/Tryna make sure your core fans never heard of you niggas/They don't wanna hear not one more noun or verb from you niggas." Kendrick signed off, crowning himself the king of New York.

"Control" resurrected the competitive nature of hiphop in the space of those eight lines. The spirit of Kool Moe Dee murdering Busy Bee with a fusillade of rhymes onstage at Harlem World comes alive in those lines. The essence of the Cold Crush Brothers battling the Fantastic Romantic Five on that same storied stage floats through those lines. Hiphop hadn't seen any real contention between rappers since Jay-Z and Nas went through a war of the words in 2001. General unfriendliness existed between Azealia Banks and Iggy Azalea, between Nicki Minaj and Lil' Kim as well. But the audacity of Kendrick Lamar insulting Big Sean and rapper Jay Electronica, who'd also added instantly overlooked verses to "Control," on their own posse track became the talk of hiphop for weeks.

Some of the song's targeted MCs sounded off on Twitter.

**King Push** ✓
@PUSHA_T

I hear u loud and clear my nigga... @kendricklamar

♡ 14.8K   11:44 PM - Aug 12, 2013                                    ❶

💬 44.3K people are talking about this                               ❯

**Big K.R.I.T.** ✓
@BIGKRIT

"This is Gladiator Shit"...Gotta give the people what they want .

♡ 637   11:50 PM - Aug 12, 2013                                     ❶

💬 3,404 people are talking about this                              ❯

At least twenty-four different rappers took to the internet with freestyle response records of their own, including J. Cole, Meek Mill, A$AP Ferg, and Lupe Fiasco. Most responders inserted themselves into the narrative just for the attention; they weren't even mentioned, well-known, or genuinely offended by "Control." By the time I interviewed Kendrick Lamar for an *Ebony* cover story in the spring of 2015, TDE forbid media to ask him about the verse anymore. But two weeks after "Control" detonated, Power 106 questioned him about the seriousness of the song reigniting the type of East Coast vs. West Coast feud blamed for the deaths of Tupac Shakur and Christopher Wallace (aka Biggie Smalls). He answered:

**It'll never be like that again where two coasts [fight]. Not on my behalf. Not while I'm doing this. And I think the OGs of the game would want that anyway. They'd want that competitive nature back and no bloodshed over it, you feel me? I'm way too wise and I'm way too polished to not get caught up in the hype of the media. But what I'm scared of is cats that's not polished, and they getting caught up in what they Twitter responses is saying and what they're homies around them saying, and people gassing them up. And they try to take it to the next level. Nah, that's not G. That's not gangsta...**

**I respect the legends in the game. I respect people who done it before me, people that lost they lives over this. So because of what they laid down, I'm gon' try and go ten times harder and breathe it and live it. And that's the whole point of the whole verse.**

Kendrick never seemed shook by the Pandora's box he'd opened, but he'd never been the target of so many slings and arrows from other rappers either. Lupe Fiasco called him insane and childish, dissing Kendrick for putting himself in the same league as Nas and Jay-Z. Sixteen-year-old Stro faulted the five-and-a-half-foot MC for having a Napoleon complex. Papoose attacked his manhood, accusing Kendrick, Kanye, and Drake of supposedly acting feminine and wearing womanly clothes. Kendrick didn't hit back at any of them.

"I didn't really have anything to say about it. It just sounded like an ambitious thought to me," Drake finally said in response to "Control," two weeks after its release. "That's all it was. I know good and well that Kendrick's not murdering me, at all, in any platform. So when that day presents itself, I guess we can revisit the topic," he told *Billboard*. "That verse, he's giving people moments," he said weeks afterward in a public interview at New York University. "That verse was a moment to talk about. Are you listening to it now? At this point? I can't wait to see what he does, because now it's time to show and prove. Consistency. It's been like one album. Consistency is, make more than one album. I look forward to seeing what he does. He's super fucking talented."

But between those statements, Drake released "The Language," a preview single from his September 2013 album, *Nothing Was the Same*. Listeners took the song's very first lines—"I don't know why they been lyin'/But your shit is not that inspirin' "—as a stab at Kendrick, similar to Jay-Z baiting Nas ("what you tryin' to kick, knowledge?") on "Takeover." Drake never mentions Kendrick in any of his songs, before or after "Control." When it comes to the art of the subliminal dis though, "The Language" launched a cold war between hiphop's greatest postmillennial MCs that's lasted for years.

That October, the BET Hip Hop Awards gave a live platform to ScHoolboy Q, Jay Rock, Ab-Soul, Isaiah Rashad, and Kendrick Lamar to run roughshod over the beat to Mobb Deep's "Shook Ones (Part II)." Other performances come to mind first when considering Kendrick and his impressive award show routines, but the raw energy of the TDE cypher reflects street-corner emceeing more than any Grammy or talk-show set he's ever done. With many a hard act to follow, Kendrick still manages to devour all the space in the room by the time Isaiah Rashad passes him the microphone. "Nothing's been the same since they dropped 'Control,' and tucked a sensitive rapper back in his pajama clothes," he spat midway through, making for subliminal dis number two.

I was an intern fresh out of college when *Vibe* put together its first issue in 1993, a black-and-white, Richard Avedon–like headshot of Snoop Dogg gracing the cover. A Time Warner venture with Quincy Jones, *Vibe* took a more polished approach to the hiphop music, culture, and politics that *The Source* had already been documenting in magazine form since 1990. The gangster rap that first inspired Kendrick Lamar to become an MC reached a fever pitch with Snoop's debut album, *Doggystyle*, making him perfect for the magazine's inaugural issue. Another print media casualty of the internet by the twenty-first century, *Vibe*'s final physical issue came twenty years later: from opening with Snoop Doggy Dogg in its premiere issue to closing with Drake on the cover of its last. Questioned about the Kendrick beef in the magazine's final December 2013 cover story interview, Drake inevitably mentioned "Control":

Where it became an issue is that I was rolling out an album while that verse was still bubbling, so my album rollout became about this thing. What am I supposed to say? Nah, we'll be buddy-buddy? Mind you, I never once said he's a bad guy [or] I don't like him. I think he's a fucking genius in his own right, but I also stood my ground as I should. And with that came another step, which then I have to realize I'm being baited and I'm not gonna fall. [Michael] Jordan doesn't have to play pickup to prove that he could ball, no offense. But I'm not gonna give you the chance to shake me necessarily, 'cause I feel great. There's no real issue.

He's going to do what he has to do, like the BET [cypher]. But again, it's not enough for me to go. We haven't seen each other, but I'm sure we'll see each other and it'll be cool. And if it's not, then I guess that's how our story unfolds.

*"Kendrick's continuing the legacy and the work that the greats have in a space where it's not valued anymore. The reason why we look at Kendrick and we marvel at the shit he's doing—his lyricism, his output, his consistency—is because he doesn't have anyone who's out there pushing him. The game is about influence, competition, and impetus. That's what it's always been based on, even when it's friendly. And the fact of the matter is, who's pushing Kendrick? Have you ever heard stories of athletes that create lies in their head to create a competition with somebody who doesn't even have beef with them, just so they can motivate themselves to push ahead? That's kind of the space that Kendrick is in. 'Cause who's pushing him? Is Drake really pushing Kendrick? No."*

—DART ADAMS

The third MC of the new millennium to mature from an acclaimed mixtape moment to multimillions of downloaded albums is J. Cole. After dropping *The Come Up*, *The Warm Up*, and *Friday Night Lights* in the early days of DatPiff file sharing, North Carolina's Jermaine Cole sparked a friendship with K-Dot early in their careers. Their long-rumored joint project has as much of a Loch Ness monster aspect to it in hiphop folklore as Dr. Dre's *Detox* album. As the first name mentioned on "Control," J. Cole didn't respond until guesting on a Justin Timberlake remix ("TKO") that November. Setting the stage about a lover playing the infamous verse on her smartphone at Cole's house, he eventually concludes: "In case this is war, then I load up on all ammunition/If a nigga want problems, my trigger's on auto/I'll make sure that nobody miss him."

A full year after "Control," performing at Drake's fifth annual OVO Fest in Toronto, J. Cole brought out the festival host during his set. "Shout-out my nigga Kendrick Lamar," Drake said before sixteen thousand fans at the Molson Canadian Amphitheatre. "Kendrick was on my album, we went on tour . . . That's one of the hardest niggas alive. He should be standing right [here]. There's a lot of kings in this shit, so shout-out to Kendrick and shout-out my brother J. Cole!"

Drake's public burying of their passive-aggressive conflict should've quashed everything. For some reason, that's not what happened.

Tupac Shakur is dead. Yesterday, waiting at The Source for Roger and Teresa to dress for a D'Angelo/Giorgio Armani party, I was on the phone with Frances up at the University of Rochester. Dave Mays walked through the conference room and told me Tupac was dead; he was plugged 4 times in the chest 7 days ago after the Tyson fight. Roger, Teresa & I were just in the room together watching an X-rated clip for "How Do U Want It" and "Hit 'Em Up." I felt overall just a feeling of wasted potential. Tupac was James Dean—he could have had a long career in film and with Death Row. We were approached outside the Armory by a New York Post writer about Tupac's death, but our comments didn't make the paper.

—a journal, September 14, 1996

On March 9, 1997, Christopher George Latore Wallace—the beloved bad boy Biggie Smalls, a.k.a. the Notorious B.I.G.—was pronounced dead at 1:15 a.m. at Cedars-Sinai Medical Center in Los Angeles, of gunshots from a drive-by shooting following a *Vibe* party. Early that Sunday morning, I rolled out of bed in the Jersey City apartment of my girlfriend to walk her terrier. (She was in L.A., at the party.) I phoned my answering machine to check the messages back at my own place in Brooklyn, two blocks down from 226 St. James Place where Big grew up. My heart dropped.

Dad called. My closest homeboy called. My girlfriend called, distraught with the details, from right outside the Peterson Automotive Museum where Biggie had been killed. I was twenty-six and had been chipping away at music journalism for three years. Big was twenty-four and the king of New York. His instantly classic *Life After Death* dropped two weeks later; I'd already reviewed it for the now-defunct *Rap Pages* magazine, in an issue sporting photographer Barron Claiborne's legendary portrait of Biggie: crimson-tinged, golden crown cocked to the side. The memory of Tupac Shakur's senseless murder less than seven months prior was still fresh on everyone's spirit.

Come March 16, hundreds of mourners stood outside the Frank E. Campbell Funeral Chapel near East 81st Street on Madison Avenue. It was the Sunday following Biggie's murder. Police officers held back throngs of fans outside. Many hopped the train to Brooklyn once the funeral procession started rolling.

The self-righteous personality streak of my twenties in full effect, I didn't join the thousands of boom-box-carrying, placard-waving rap lovers—both young and old, overwhelmingly black and brown—clogging the streets of St. James Place that afternoon. In a basement garden apartment two streets away on Grand Avenue, I stayed in bed. I'd seen Big perform at a Howard University homecoming ("May see me in D.C. at Howard Homecoming," he once rhymed on "Kick in the Door"), again at a *Vibe* anniversary party, and once walking down 23rd Street near the Tunnel nightclub with Faith Evans—an after-party for the Source Awards. But we'd never met. Standing out in the freezing cold waiting for his hearse to roll down the street seemed like ambulance chasing to me. I was wrong. Turns out it wasn't morbid or opportunistic at all; it was a celebration.

My gut made me venture outdoors, my stomach specifically. Around lunchtime I hit the Key Food supermarket on Fulton Street, around the corner from St. James Place. (Even before his death, the store hung a framed photo of our local hero on the wall, right past the cash registers.) Moving through the sidewalks wasn't easy; I took to the street. The multitude of folks made up a living, breathing memorial shrine: candles, flowers, cardboard signs, B.I.G. T-shirts for sale. I spotted other music writers who'd loved, met, and written of Biggie the past three years. There were TV camera trucks too. Everyone watching, waiting, anticipating. I ducked back inside, firing up my oven and Tricky's *Nearly God*.

And then, at 2:10, the motorcade arrived: eight stretch limousines and about thirty flowered cars. Turning onto St. James Place toward Fulton Ave, a JFK-worthy cavalcade of mourners—his mother, Voletta Wallace; Sean Combs, Faith Evans, Junior M.A.F.I.A.'s Lil' Cease, Lil' Kim, and more—accompanied the Notorious B.I.G. in his final touchdown to Planet Brooklyn. "Hypnotize" galvanized the crowd into dancing, shouting, and other fitful bursts of exaltation. But then the New York Police Department got antsy. The hearse took its leave of the neighborhood only five minutes earlier, but cops wanted near-immediate dispersal. A few heated words led to pepper spray from the police and the separation of everyone assembled.

Hungry for spectacle, the next day's *New York Times* led with "On Rap Star's Final Ride, Homage Is Marred by a Scuffle." *Times* reporter Julia Campbell was arrested and charged with disorderly conduct, along with nine others. As long and strong as the memorial lasted, the streets of Clinton Hill were completely cleared fifteen minutes after Biggie's pass-through.

My own suffering in silence sprung from the shock of it all more than anything else. Big and Tupac were two of the most talented, personally magnetic MCs of the time; were Snoop Dogg, Sean Combs, or any other rappers any safer? Blaring Tricky and Alison Moyet's "Make a Change" from my small, *Purple Rain*–ish basement apartment, I mourned Biggie in private with some Chocolate Thai cannabis and chocolate chip cookies. That day, he belonged to Brooklyn, belonged to us all.

**184**

# 5.

By Halloween 2014, the "Control" verse wasn't on hiphop's collective radar much anymore. Drake had come out publicly at his own OVO Fest to praise Kendrick's king status and retire the drama. But then the latest Jay Rock single, "Pay for It," came out of nowhere with a Kendrick verse referencing Drake all over again: "I tell 'em all to hail King Kendrick, resurrectin' my vengeance/Been dissectin' your motormouth 'til I break down the engine." Why? Perhaps the verse was recorded before Drake's August proclamation at OVO. Or something else private between the two, outside the purview of anything fans or media were privy to. But the jab, still somewhat subliminal, was clear enough: Drake had called himself "the kid with the motormouth" on "The Language." Now Kendrick threatened to break down the engine of that motor. "Endin' our friendship, baby," he continued, "I'd rather die alone."

Death actually isn't an option anyone in hiphop has any interest in exploring. In 2018 the Prison Policy Initiative, a criminal justice–oriented public policy think tank, reported that the murder rate for black men is consistently higher than the murder rate for men of all other racial and ethnic groups has ever been. African-American males are already killed disproportionately. Some of them emcee. An atmosphere of ambiguity when it comes to the motives behind these murders—made ambiguous because of conflicts with other rappers—can only hurt the chances of the homicides being solved. Neither Biggie's nor Tupac's ever was.

Rapper Nipsey Hussle died from multiple gunshot wounds in March 2019, killed in L.A. by someone he'd had an altercation with earlier in the day. Barely nine months prior, XXXTentacion, a rising rapper from Florida, was fatally shot numerous times in a robbery outside a Deerfield Beach motorbike dealership. Subliminal jabs have largely replaced the kind of direct hits that songs like Nas's "Ether" or

Remy Ma's "Shether" represented because black life is precarious enough without MCs giving overzealous fans or former gang affiliates inspiration to travel down deadly paths. Why Kendrick came for Drake again after his OVO olive branch isn't known. But the reason why he continued not to name Drake explicitly is fairly obvious.

The tit-for-tat starts to read like a bullet-point Wikipedia list. In February 2015 Drake released *If You're Reading This It's Too Late*, a so-called commercial mixtape, with a few lines on "Used To" that listeners construed as a Kendrick dis: "They gon' say your name on them airwaves/ They gon' hit you up right after like it's only rap." Translation: Drake encountered Kendrick at the Barclays Center in Brooklyn for the MTV Video Music Awards the week after "Control" dropped in 2013. He told his September '13 NYU audience:

**I know that verse had no malice behind it, because I saw him five days later at the VMAs and it was all love. He didn't come on there on some wild "I'm in New York, fuck everybody, don't look at me." It was one of those things, I almost wished he had come in there on that shit, because I kind of lost a little respect for the sentiment of the verse. If it's really "fuck everybody," then it needs to be "fuck everybody." It can't be halfway for the sake of the people.**

Kendrick's next oblique mention of his rival came on *To Pimp a Butterfly*'s "King Kunta" in March 2015, wherein he takes rappers to task for employing ghostwriters: "I can dig rappin'," he says, invoking the 1973 James Brown line, "but a rapper with a ghostwriter? What the fuck happened?" While Kendrick and Drake spent years soft-footing around each other, Philadelphia battle rapper Meek Mill went for Drake's jugular later that summer claiming on Twitter that an aspiring MC named Quentin Miller wrote some of his rhymes. Miller is indeed credited on several songs from *If You're Reading This It's Too Late*, and his reference track rapping on an earlier version of Drake's "10 Bands" soon surfaced on hiphop radio. The conflama stood Kendrick's verse in even starker relief. Beyoncé singing lyrics written by, say, Frank Ocean doesn't faze the public the way that Jay-Z performing someone else's material would. An underlying assumption exists that rappers are poets, and if your poetry isn't actually your own, then what value do you have? Though a handful of MCs, from Eazy-E to Kanye West, have used ghostwriters at different points, being accused of the practice is a major insult.

Embroiled in controversy, Drake never responded to "King Kunta," subliminally or otherwise, and dropped his cold war completely. Around then, Kendrick mentor Dr. Dre emerged from retirement with his first album in sixteen years, summer 2015's *Compton*. "Still I got enemies giving me energy, I don't wanna fight now/Subliminally sent to me all of this hate, I thought I was holding the mic down," Kendrick complains on the album's "Darkside/Gone." Any further thinly veiled disses from Drake went unreleased. In that sense, he folded like the Soviet Union—no peace treaty, no détente. Instead he reserved his lyrical ICBMs for Meek Mill, launching two straightforward, back-to-back dis records that earned him a pretty uncontested win.

As a postscript, Dr. Michael Eric Dyson—minister, cultural critic, professor—taught an undergrad class at Georgetown University in the fall of 2019 entitled Sociology and Culture: Drake. As much as I believe there is to unpack about Kendrick Lamar, professor Dyson found at least as much to explore about Kendrick's one-time nemesis. And just as MCs have come for the head of King Kendrick, rappers who believe Drake wears the crown and doesn't deserve to have stormed his castle too. In 2018 rapper Pusha-T attacked Drake in the hard-core way certain bloodthirsty rap fans hoped Kendrick would. He indicted Drake by name for using ghostwriters; he exposed a questionable photo of him wearing blackface to all the internet; he even broke an unwritten rule by outing Drake as a dad, dragging a baby into the battle. By going super ugly, Pusha-T "won." All things considered, both Kendrick and Drake seem more honorable for keeping their beef far above that level.

# 6.

Once upon a time at a recent Bronx block party, vendors behind a metal folding table sold CDs of 1970s mixes by DJ Grandmaster Flash right next to stacked T-shirts with the printed slogan *FUCK YOU, I RHYME BETTER*. The motto comes from an obscure rap song from the turn of the millennium, but it sums up the spirit of hip-hop in a nutshell. No hopeful wannabe MC starts scribbling rhymes in a notebook to perform without the confidence that s/he might be better at rhythm, rhyme, tone, cadence, and content than the next rapper. I rhyme better than you has always been embedded in rappers' source code.

In the digital age, rappers going at one another on social media makes the art of MC battling seem like a ghost of its former self. Shyne (an MC most famous for getting incarcerated after firing gunshots while in a club with Sean Combs and Jennifer Lopez back in 1999) voiced his strong opinion of *good kid, m.A.A.d city* on Twitter the night of its release: "Kendrick Lamar is talented with a lot of potential but his album is traaaaash! I expected *doggy style* or *the chronic*. I got a product that was trash. I looked forward to hearing an instant classic from *good kid*. Trash!" Shyne found himself on the wrong side of history pretty instantly. Rapper Lupe Fiasco used the same platform in 2018 to tell over a million followers "KDot is not a top tier lyricist to me and my standards when it comes to punchlines and bars. His overall lyrics are good his stories phenomenal BUT punchline entendre lyrically I don't see it." He later deleted the tweet and apologized live on Instagram. Jay Electronica drove through Miami in the winter of 2016 broadcasting live on Periscope. When a fan asked him to play some Kendrick Lamar music, he said, "Fuck that." After giving respect to the early single "Cartoons & Cereal," he threw his shade: "Other than that, we don't know what these lames is talking about. Kendrick would tell you himself he couldn't body me. Kendrick is my son. Kendrick is my baby. Kendrick wishes he could be me." No one expects unanimous acclaim for any artist. Kendrick Lamar's artistry registers as exceptional when measured by any barometer. But Michelangelo hated Leonardo di Vinci. Many considered Motown legends Mary Wilson and Diana Ross archenemies after (and during) their time in the Supremes. When the tides of rock and roll turned away hair metal bands, the attitude of Guns N' Roses toward Nirvana looked remarkably like the cruelty of jocks toward geeks at any given high school. Artists, hiphop or otherwise, aren't going to like one another all the time—for reasons rooted in self-doubt, resentment, rivalry, and whatever all else. Why should creatives be any different than the rest of us?

CHAPTER 6

# DNA

## 1.

The Bronx and Brooklyn didn't get along that great when I was young. Kids from each borough repped their section of New York City back then like we owned equity in the concrete of the Bronx, Manhattan, Queens, Staten Island, and Brooklyn streets. Early Spike Lee movies like *She's Gotta Have It* and *Mo' Better Blues* seduced me to cross the Brooklyn Bridge for my first apartment in the mid-1990s. Truth be told, the young, gifted, and black college grads planting roots in those Fort Greene and Clinton Hill neighborhoods full of brownstones and bodegas were the first to gentrify the area.

My first encounter with the decade's spoken-word movement took place at Brooklyn Moon, a lounge/restaurant where poets took over the open microphone every Friday. Before the world knew *Baduizm*, twenty-five-year-old Erykah Badu lived across the street and strolled down Fulton Street anonymously on a daily basis. Her head wraps and ankh jewelry and Afrocentric style matched the overall vibe of that hood back then; that is to say, she barely stood out. She knew my best friend's roommate from Dallas, which is how we met in 1996, at a Brooklyn house party full of incense, poetry, and marijuana. She'd perform "On & On," the Grammy-winning, number-one R&B hit, in my bestie's living room in between all the other local singers and MCs. After the world knew her name, BET cameras set up in the same apartment to capture Badu in her natural habitat of black bohemia. (I say this with some sarcasm. We were all just in our twenties, trying to live our best lives.)

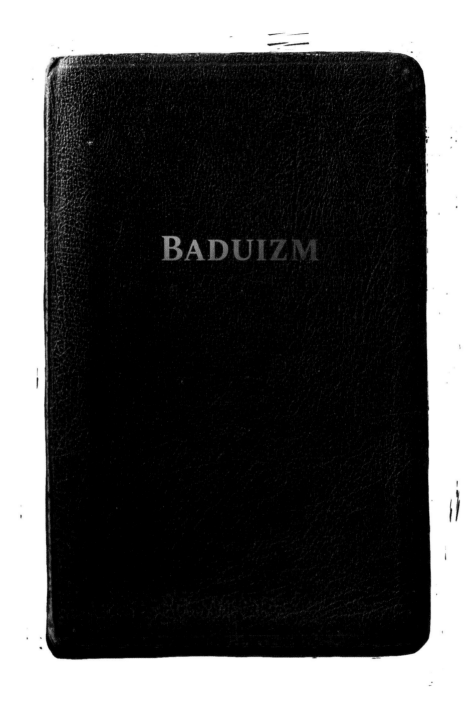

I profiled Erykah in *The Source* before her first single, when she was only famous for appearing in the video of a D'Angelo remix. She knew my editor from her old high school and asked me not to tell him she smoked, while sitting in my Chevrolet rolling a cigar for the interview. *Baduizm* finally dropped in February 1997. At the end of some Brooklyn Moon function, I came to her with a positive *Rolling Stone* review under my arm. "Perhaps the first thing you notice about Erykah Badu is her uncanny vocal similarity to Billie Holiday—from the very beginning of *Baduizm*, Badu's debut, the boho chanteuse's timbre and inflections recall Lady Day. By the end of the album, however, it's clear that Badu is from the Diana Ross school of Billie Holiday imitation: Like Ross in her portrayal of Holiday in *Lady Sings the Blues*, Badu is mainly interested in just being herself." She hated the piece and told me, without looking at the byline. It was the first *Rolling Stone* review I ever wrote.

The takeaway here is that Billie Holiday was very much a part of the conversation at the beginning of Badu's career. Her first album hosted jazz bassist Ron Carter and trumpeter Roy Hargrove; she sang smoky jazz club freestyles like "Afro." Her last name was a scat in and of itself. Her band even opened live shows playing Miles Davis's "So What." Badu's future material reached past that pigeonholed comfort zone of the jazzy hiphop singer, and others made whole careers out

*"Whether or not they wholly intend to, certain figures in popular music neatly attach themselves to the classic hero's journey that Joseph Campbell identified in his comparative studies of mythology. Dylan is one, and so is Kendrick: young men with prodigious talent touching upon cultural profundities by trying to figure themselves out. Both also have a strong sense of history and are unapologetic about declaring themselves part of it. And both project an appealing masculinity that doesn't seem to be tragic, or deeply harmful to women—you might even, at times, call their music feminist."*
—ANN POWERS

*"Everybody was making 'concept albums' in the '60s and '70s: Sun Ra, Ornette, Coltrane, Miles, Parliament, the Art Ensemble of Chicago, Earth, Wind & Fire, Rick James. After came Prince: Dirty Mind, Controversy, and 1999 are all part of that conceptual pantheon. But I don't think the 'concept' is always literally thematic à la Marvin Gaye—sometimes it's sonic and tribal, à la Mandrill, and Rufus with Chaka Khan. I think* To Pimp a Butterfly *is as revolutionary as* What's Going On *was in bridging the three realms of concept, sonics, and thematics: a breakthrough on multiple levels of musical, political, and thematic continuity and innovation. Conceptual agitprop at its finest, but grounded in life and empathy."*
—GREG TATE

of it. But in her earliest days, it was clear that she stood on the shoulders of certain artists who'd come before: she sang covers of songs by Roy Ayers, Chaka Khan, Bob Marley, Atlantic Starr. One of those covers was the Motown duet, "Your Precious Love."

Twelve months after releasing the '90s soul staple *Brown Sugar*, D'Angelo met Erykah and me in a midtown Manhattan recording studio to lay down "Your Precious Love" for a soundtrack album. His debut CD married hiphop to rhythm and blues in a way that made critics want to name a whole new genre to describe it. The former rapper from Richmond, Virginia, shared his Newport cigarettes and spoke thoughtfully about that new sound, brushing ashes from his baggy jeans and smiling a lot at his singing partner. At twenty-two, D'Angelo had also made clear which musicians ran through his DNA by singing covers on soundtracks and in concert: the Ohio Players, Smokey Robinson, Prince, Eddie Kendricks. He showed up that very afternoon to play the Marvin Gaye to Erykah's Tammi Terrell on "Your Precious Love." Fans who loved *Brown Sugar* and 2000's *Voodoo* would later argue whether the burden of living up to those greats—Prince and Marvin Gaye especially—accounted for the extreme delay between *Voodoo* and 2014's *Black Messiah*.

Before his extended hiatus, D'Angelo appeared on another duet in 1998: "Nothing Really Matters," a heavenly ballad from *The Miseducation of Lauryn Hill.* Sampling breakbeats and hooks of music from older sources has belonged to the hiphop generation since "Rapper's Delight" borrowed from Chic's "Good Times"—earlier even. During the 1990s, that generational instinct overflowed into soul music. So-called neo-soul and hiphop soul sampled the very spirit of black music titans like Chaka Khan, Billie Holiday, Marvin Gaye, Nina Simone, and others, filtering it through premillennial hiphop and blessing music lovers with the likes of Mary J. Blige, Erykah Badu, D'Angelo, and former Fugees rapper Lauryn Hill. As the new-wave R&B singers of the time, they helped birth future eclectic soul to come from Janelle Monáe, Frank Ocean, H.E.R., SZA, and more. But there seemed to be a price to pay.

Though Erykah Badu continued recording regularly, D'Angelo released only three albums in the span of nineteen years, and Lauryn Hill never released another studio album at all. So many admiring fans were ready to embrace them as our generation's answer to Stevie Wonder, Marvin Gaye, and Prince that who could blame them for the agoraphobia? By contrast, filling the shoes of Michael Jackson hasn't intimidated Beyoncé from becoming the Queen of Pop as far as anyone can tell. She's not a child of the '70s like Badu, Hill, or D'Angelo either; like Kendrick Lamar, she was born in the 1980s, so maybe the bravery is generational. For an *Interview* cover story in 2013, Erykah once asked Kendrick Lamar about his influences. He admitted to studying Jay-Z, Nas, Tupac, and Biggie, confessing that he might never reach Eminem or Jay-Z's level of excellence. But he forged forward and gave it a shot anyway. The outcome gave us one of the greatest artists of the millennium thus far. Kendrick told us all about the royalty inside his DNA—the power, poison, pain, and joy, the hustle, ambition and flow. He reaches further through his artistry by standing on the shoulders of giants.

# 2.

There's not much consensus over what constitutes a concept album. A simple Facebook hivemind request—"What's your favorite concept album by a black artist?"—yielded everything imaginable. Many mentioned Stevie Wonder's *Journey Through the Secret Life of Plants*, Millie Jackson's *Caught Up*, Beyoncé's *Lemonade*, Janet Jackson's *Rhythm Nation 1814*, Jay-Z's *4:44*, and Tyler, the Creator's *Igor*. Jazz albums without any lyrics at all made a few followers' lists: Miles Davis's *Bitches Brew*, *Journey Into Satchidananda* by Alice Coltrane, *A Love Supreme* by John Coltrane. Critic Ann Powers mentioned Duke Ellington's *A Drum Is a Woman*. Professor Michael Eric Dyson listed Curtis Mayfield's *Superfly*, OutKast's *Speakerboxxx/The Love Below*, and Maxwell's *Urban Hang Suite*. Novelist Marlon James said *De La Soul Is Dead*, Janelle Monáe's *The ArchAndroid*, and *Black Music* by Chocolate Genius. Other records came up that don't really have any single central narrative running throughout: ScHoolboy Q's *Oxymoron*, Prince's *Sign o' the Times* and *1999*, Janelle Monáe's *Dirty Computer*. Some said (rightfully so) that Sun Ra, Parliament, and Funkadelic only made concept albums.

What's Going On and good kid, m.A.A.d city surfaced several times too.

Talk about Kendrick Lamar's musical lineage and Tupac Shakur is his most obvious forefather. Kendrick grew up idolizing him; he crashed the set of his "California Love" video as a little boy; he dialogues with Pac beyond the grave at the end of "Mortal Man," etc. But Kendrick's artistry deserves an evaluation that considers him in the context of Nina Simone, Fela Anikulapo-Kuti, and other singer-songwriters who addressed freedom, equality, and Afro-pessimism in their work. His work shares as much of its sensibilities with Marvin Gaye's discography as any rapper he ever put on a pedestal, starting with the idea of the concept album.

Concept albums are generally understood to be a cycle of songs expressing a particular theme or idea. By that wide-ranging definition, any R&B album speaking about love from beginning to end arguably qualifies. But real concept albums run deeper. When David Bowie takes on the identity of an interstellar alien unfamiliar with Earth's ways and mores to critique them as the ultimate outsider (see *The Rise and Fall of Ziggy Stardust and the Spiders from Mars*), that's what we're talking about. Or *The Wall*, Pink Floyd's double-album about depression and isolation through the eyes of a jaded rock star. *Lemonade* and *4:44* are conceptual bookends about both sides of infidelity in a marriage from Beyoncé and Jay-Z's individual points of view. Kendrick Lamar has become no less famous for his concept albums than a classic rock band like The Who. *Section.80* deals with the reverberating effects of Ronald Reagan—era ideologies on the generation born in the 1980s. A few songs use recurring characters—the sex worker Keisha, the lovelorn Tammy—to make various points about the social dynamics of black American women. Kendrick has a loose understanding of Reaganomics, but *Section.80* still critiques the negative impact of the conservative president's racist policies. Theories about the government flooding inner cities with drugs and guns during the decade float throughout the album too. *Good kid, m.A.A.d city* comes even tighter with a story line: a day in the life of a kid from Compton, who nearly gets sidelined into gangbanging before a spiritual redemption pulls him back onto the right path. *To Pimp a Butterfly* swirls around survivor's guilt, depression, black nationalism, and the temptations nipping at the heels of superstardom. He introduced more characters on both those albums:

sexy Sherane, Lucy/Lucifer. Keisha even makes a comeback on *good kid, m.A.A.d city*, as if everyone he rhymes about belongs to the same near-cinematic universe. At its beginning and at the climax, *DAMN.* brackets its songs with a mysterious murder, using Kid Capri ad-libs, complaints about not being prayed for, and recurring vocal refrains from Bēkon about wickedness and weakness to gel the record together.

My great-grandmother passed away the morning Marvin Gaye died; I was thirteen. Because of our family tragedy going on at the same time, the death of Marvin Gaye—one of my father's personal favorites—became just a post-script to the day. But my dad had seen Marvin over fifteen times in concert. He was a teenage gofer for The Temptations (he's literally seen them perform live over a hundred times), a Harlem city kid who practically lived at the Apollo Theater growing up. Motown felt sacrosanct in our house, a microcosm of most African-American baby boomer households across the country. *What's Going On, Let's Get It On, I Want You, Here, My Dear* and many a Marvin Gaye mixtape got heavy rotation at home, in the car, and on family road trips down South. The omnipresence of his music back then must mirror what Kendrick experienced in his wonder years too. He constantly mentions his parents' love for The Isley Brothers and Marvin Gaye in early interviews, and so all those soulful concept albums run through Kendrick's blood.

*"Most jazz/hiphop fusions end up shorting on the jazz and the emceeing fronts. Kendrick took up the challenge of adapting your flow to the looser, less regimented time of a jazz rhythm section—especially on 'For Free? (Interlude).' His agility in jumping onto a swinging free bop beat with flavor and ferocity was phenomenal. To Pimp a Butterfly is the most satisfying fusion of the two genres because it's led by an MC who's musical enough to collaborate and even challenge his jazz player cohort and rip with his full powers as a creative MC. Outside of Freestyle Fellowship, and except for A Tribe Called Quest's interaction with Ron Carter, we've never heard one of our best MCs sound so comfortable with live improvising musicians or produce hiphop classics with them."*
—GREG TATE

**203**

*"I think it's fruitful to examine the connection between Kendrick and Lauryn Hill at her peak—both were acting as rap insiders who were also moral agents, people raised on hiphop and in love with it, who also had been affected negatively by its hierarchies and myths. I'd consider Kendrick's work in relationship to Marvin's through the lens of Lauryn. Hill and Lamar were younger than Gaye was when they made the leap into concept albums, and much earlier in their careers. I think Hill was thinking about the legacy of Gaye and Aretha Franklin, and Lamar was thinking about the legacy of Hill."*

—ANN POWERS

*Sgt. Pepper's Lonely Hearts Club Band*, that all-important Beatles album, gets praised as the most famous concept album of all time—the concept is the group masquerading as the fictional band of the title. But the idea only lasts for three of the thirteen songs. Released four years later, *What's Going On*—the highest-ranking record on *Rolling Stone*'s Greatest Albums of All Time list—explores its own themes far more thoroughly. Inspired by his brother Frankie's tour in the Vietnam War, Marvin recorded an album from the viewpoint of a returning veteran struggling with injustice, poverty, drug abuse, and racism in the world he returns to. His next album exploring an idea from start to finish, *Let's Get It On*, centered on erotica, love, and seduction, as did *I Want You*. These records contained some of the biggest hits of his career: "Mercy Mercy Me (The Ecology)," "Inner City Blues (Make Me Wanna Holler)," "Distant Lover," "After the Dance," every single title track. The backstory to *Here, My Dear* carried more weight than the album itself for many years. Married to Anna Gordy, older sister of Motown founder Berry Gordy, for fourteen years, Gaye eventually went through a divorce that stipulated half the royalties from his next album be forwarded to his ex-wife. So he turned in the double-album *Here, My Dear*, an hour-plus meditation on love gone sour. There were no hits, the record getting much more respect from fans and critics

204

in the decades since 1978. But Marvin Gaye, whose records played nonstop in the Lamar household of Compton in the 1990s, pioneered the type of concept records that Kendrick put his own hiphop twist on with most of his albums.

Have a look on the internet at Kendrick sitting in the grassy back-yard of Rick Rubin's minimalist Malibu home in late 2016, talking to the legendary producer about the creative process while wearing an orange knit cap identical to Marvin Gaye's famous red fisherman beanie (see *Let's Get It On*). Now, with that visual reference fresh in mind, consider Kendrick's Black Lives Matter anthem "Alright" against *What's Going On* as a soul music protest album. Nigerian Afrobeat pioneer Fela Kuti wove social commentary throughout many of his songs, as did reggae godhead Bob Marley. But another parallel between Kendrick and Marvin Gaye is that the breadth of their output spans out way beyond what hiphop would call con-scious records. When artists are typecast as exclusively conscious, it normally doesn't bode well for them commercially. (Fela and Marley existed in their own special universes.) And so a final lesson learned by Kendrick from Marvin might have been to switch things up. Though millennial ladies love cool Drake, Kendrick quietly recorded nearly as many tributes to the fairer sex: "LOVE.," "These Walls," "Poetic Justice," etc. The topical diversity suits him as well as it did the author of "Let's Get It On." The narrator of Marvin Gaye's "Trouble Man" had come up just as hard as the lead character of *good kid, m.A.A.d city*; the storyteller behind *What's Going On* held just as many questions about black people and white supremacy as the one who rhymed "Alright." But all that goes down easier with the occasional "Got to Give It Up" or "All the Stars." From one trouble man to another, Kendrick wears the knit cap well.

**3.**

I discovered James Brown three times.

    We've all been told stories from our baby-hoods that we don't directly remember. One of mine involves a favorite toy, Curtis Mayfield's *Superfly* soundtrack, and how much I schlepped around the scratched vinyl album, slapping it onto my Fisher-Price turntable in between diaper changes. I vaguely recall my great-grandma's teen-age foster kids in the South Bronx performing *Soul Train* dances to their Jackson 5 singles. But my first memory of a seven-inch vinyl single, the one with the large donut hole in the middle, goes back to my thirteen-year-old uncle's bed-room and "The Payback" by James Brown. I re-member him pointing out the line "I don't know karate, but I know ca-razy" as something funny that I could wrap my three-year-old mind around. (Unlike J.B., I did know karate, having already seen Bruce Lee's *Return of the Dragon*.)

    Fourteen years passed and my father took me to see James Brown play the Apollo the same summer I left for college. The Godfather of Soul meant a few different things to me by then. In my teenage years I worshipped at the purple altar of Prince, who had J.B.'s polyrhythmic funk run-

*"What one generation must pursue deliberately, the next can pursue in a more natural way. A Tribe Called Quest and Digable Planets incorporated jazz samples into hiphop as a way of both injecting novelty into the mix and connecting it with the long history of African-American music, but they weren't necessarily hanging out with established jazz musicians. Kendrick came to jazz without having to make a big deal of it. Lamar was walking toward jazz before it became wholly evident to his fans; he did a verse on Robert Glasper's* Black Radio *(sadly, dropped from the final version) before his own debut came out. Jazz is an underlying inspiration on that album, and when it came time for him to really show his connection to the music on* To Pimp a Butterfly, *it all felt organic."*

—ANN POWERS

**208**

ning through his DNA. I wasn't a crate digger flipping through dusty albums in downtown record stores; I was more of a six-degrees-of-separation completist. At the time, music mags reported on Prince endlessly running his band through J.B.'s "Bodyheat," and so I added that 1976 single to a mixtape with Hendrix and Staple Singers songs he also played live back then. I appreciated that Prince trained his backing bands with all the discipline and turn-on-a-dime precision of a James Brown group, docking musicians for mistakes, educating them to watch his every move onstage. But I bought my first James Brown compilation, *In the Jungle Groove*, because somewhere on there was "Funky Drummer." And "Funky Drummer" mattered to me mainly because of hiphop.

Nearly every rapper I listened to sampled Clyde Stubblefield's breakdown from "Funky Drummer": Public Enemy, Big Daddy Kane, Ultramagnetic MCs, Boogie Down Productions . . . everybody. Hiphop of the mid-'80s overflowed with bits and pieces of James Brown classics released when I was a little kid and from even before I was born. My parents had some of his records around—*Hell, Get on the Good Foot*—but outside of '70s radio, rap music introduced me to the Hardest Working Man in Show Business in a way that felt connected to the wonder years I was living through. Riding on a wave of hiphop relevance, he released his last top forty single

*"Bob Dylan, long on record as a rap fan, already predicted the coming of K-Dot, and tacitly his cultural class hierarchy vaulting Pulitzer award, in his memoir, Chronicles. Dylan: 'Ice-T, Public Enemy, N.W.A, Run-DMC. These guys definitely weren't bullshitting. They were beating drums, tearing it up, hurling horses over cliffs. They were all poets and knew what was going on. Somebody different was bound to come along sooner or later who would know that world, been born and raised with it . . . be all of it and more. Someone with a chopped topped head and a power in the community. He'd be able to balance himself on one leg on a tightrope that stretched across the universe and you'd know him when he came—there'd only be one like him. The audience would go that way and I couldn't blame them. The kind of music that Danny [Lanois] and I were making was archaic.' With Ice-T and Public Enemy laying the tracks, a new performer was bound to appear. And unlike Elvis Presley, he wouldn't be swinging his hips and staring at the lassies. He'd be doing it with hard words and he'd be working eighteen hours a day."*
—GREG TATE

the year I saw him in concert: "Static" (complete with overdubbed crackles and pops of old vinyl records, released just at the start of the compact disc revolution). The show wasn't Prince, but it was impressive.

And then I really discovered him. The ultimate James Brown collection, *Star Time*, dropped three years later and I finally knew him for the soul and funk wayfinder he'd been since the 1950s. College pregames to many a wild night out in Atlanta started at home with "Get Up, Get Into It, and Get Involved," "Talkin' Loud & Sayin' Nothing," or songs from ancillary bands, like Fred Wesley & the New J.B.s' "(It's Not the Express) It's the JB's Monaurail." Biographies, articles, and liner notes taught me about the man and the background behind some of his greatest hits. James Brown's social activism, civil rights participation, cultural politics, and overall pro-blackness paved the road for Kendrick Lamar to speed down while hanging out the window like the Joker in *The Dark Knight*.

When honoring him with a Generational Icon Award on the California State Senate floor in 2015, Senator Isadore Hall III said Kendrick "has personally donated hundreds of thousands of dollars to support sports programs, after-school programs, [and] music programs in the Compton Unified School District to help keep Compton students off the streets and in the classroom." He tends to make most donations outside the watchful eye of media, but a $50,000 contribution to his Centennial High School alma mater for their music department got good press back in 2013. Celebrity philanthropy might seem par for the course. But looking for links between Kendrick and black music icons of the past, these moves come straight out of the James Brown playbook. In 1966, J.B. released the top-five R&B hit "Don't Be a Drop-Out," encouraging youth to stick with formal education and donating the song's royalties to dropout prevention charity programs. Like Kendrick's loyalty to Compton, Mr. "Please, Please, Please" similarly hosted an annual toy giveaway in his native Augusta, Georgia, at Christmastime for fifteen years. He entitled his final single, released in 2001, "Killing Is Out, School Is In."

Following the murder of Trayvon Martin, President Barack Obama launched the racial justice initiative My Brother's Keeper in 2014, a series of mentoring and education programs for young black men. In January 2016, Kendrick Lamar appeared in a public service announcement—shooting basketball with a fresh-faced kid, shaking hands with the president in the Oval Office—throwing his support behind Obama's platform. That fourth of July, he performed "Swimming Pools (Drank)," "Money Trees," "Poetic Justice," and more at the last White House barbeque of Obama's presidency. Janelle Monáe played her own setlist that Independence Day; musicians meeting with America's head of state isn't as rare as it once was. But James Brown laid down a template again, this time through a controversial alliance with former president Richard Nixon.

"No more black stuff," Nixon said to an aide on an Oval Office tape recording from 1972. "No more blacks from now on. Just don't bring 'em in here." J.B. hadn't supported Nixon during the 1968 campaign that awarded him the presidency. But he accepted a performance slot in the Nixon inauguration's All-American Gala when invited, explaining to *Jet* magazine, "I accepted because I want to give our new president a chance to bring the people of this nation together in every respect of our national life." So he performed; Nixon didn't attend due to security concerns. By reelection time, James Brown met with Richard Nixon despite the president's reluctance, pushing for a Martin Luther King, Jr. holiday and endorsing his reelection campaign. Fans weren't happy. Nixon's conservatism and racism (other taped conversations revealed his frequent use of the word "nigger") made him a strange bedfellow for the Godfather, who dissed him with "You Can Have Watergate Just Gimme Some Bucks and I'll Be Straight" after the 1972 scandal that led to his resignation. Kendrick Lamar made far more sense by collaborating with the country's first black president, who's gone on record more than once as actually enjoying his music. But in this sense, James Brown walked so Kendrick could run. African-American musical icons like Michael Jackson, Aretha Franklin, and Beyoncé have now become far more commonplace in the White House.

## Finally, James Brown stood for black pride in the age of Black Is Beautiful,

211

something he supported again and again on songs like "Say It Loud—I'm Black and I'm Proud" and the self-empowerment anthem "I Don't Want Nobody to Give Me Nothing (Open Up the Door, I'll Get It Myself)." He mentored Reverend Al Sharpton, one of the greatest black activists of modern times. He encouraged Pan-Africanism, performing in Zaire at the famous Muhammad Ali boxing match against George Foreman; included African countries like Nigeria and Zambia on his world tours; and inspired the evolution of Afrobeat. On the night after Martin Luther King, Jr. was assassinated, his improvised speech onstage at the Boston Garden (broadcast live on local television) helped calm a grieved, angered community engaged in nationwide spates of rioting. Those are all huge footsteps to follow, but maybe more than anyone else in hiphop, Kendrick walks the same path. The Movement for Black Lives adopted his protest anthem "Alright" for themselves in 2015. His embrace of the Motherland shines through on tracks like "Momma" and "How Much a Dollar Cost," which reflect the time he spent touring South Africa in 2014. His commingling of hiphop, trap, and African gqom styles on his curated soundtrack to 2018's top-grossing *Black Panther* goes even further, pairing African musicians like Babes Wodumo and Sjava with Vince Staples, Anderson .Paak, and Jorja Smith of Great Britain. Even his orchestration of *Black Panther: The Album* harks back to James Brown soundtracks like *Black Caesar* and *Slaughter's Big Rip-Off*—though J.B. already trailed behind Curtis Mayfield, Isaac Hayes, and others when it came to recording movie music.

Still, all this proves that when Kendrick released "King Kunta" with sampled elements from James Brown's "The Payback," the nod was no accident. Kung Fu Kenny knows ca-razy.

# 4.

In the sphere of hiphop culture, Kendrick Lamar's most obvious influencer is Tupac Amaru Shakur. From his teenage days emceeing as K-Dot to his Grammy-winning albums, he's mentioned Tupac countless times. He's said that Tupac ghostwrites his lyrics on "What the Deal." Given shout-outs to Thug Life on "Death Around the Corner" and "HiiiPower." Told us to call him Pac on his remix to "I Do This." He's recorded his own "Brenda's Got a Baby" with "Keisha's Song (Her Pain)" (wherein Keisha actually listens to the Pac song within her own song), created his own Thug Life with HiiiPower. *To Pimp a Butterfly* ends with a simulated conversation between Kendrick and Tupac, on an album recorded with the tentative title *TuPaC* (*Tu Pimp a Caterpillar*). He's dreamed about Tupac—"keep doing what you're doing, don't let my music die," he told him. Game showed similar hero worship by name-dropping scores of MCs on his earliest albums, but Kendrick/Tupac is a special kind of connection. Kendrick's birthday is June 17: one day after Tupac's, but with sixteen years of separation. Kendrick was nine when Tupac died; they never met. In hiphop, only Jay-Z and Biggie Smalls—who were something like peers—had a comparable kinship, but they were contemporaries. Kendrick's connection to Tupac has been far more metaphysical.

I envied my father for living in the time of Jimi Hendrix, who died months before I was born. Each generation has its icons, and being alive to see the boisterous vivacity of Tupac Shakur's life in real time is something I feel thankful for. Some potential college roommate (it didn't work out) turned me on to his first album, *2Pacalypse Now*, back when I mainly only cared about A Tribe Called Quest and De La Soul when it came to hiphop.

His starring role in *Juice* impressed me. His first cover of *Vibe* surprised me a few

*"I think Kendrick, like Snoop, Ice Cube, and Biggie, is of that highest order—a cinematic auteur MC storyteller. By that, I mean the cats whose vocal tone alone can put you in the middle of a compelling story and conjure up the mood and mystery of a great film noir with one phrase, like 'bitch, don't kill my vibe.' They're like directors who can rhyme and give you everything a movie gives you: lights, camera, action in spellbinding verse."*
—GREG TATE

*"For me, the kind of storyteller Kendrick is starts with Stevie Wonder and 'Living for the City.' His lyricism and sense of mission feel very soulful to me. He doesn't feel so much like a trickster, like André 3000—and he's also not a movie-informed gangster type, like Biggie or Jay-Z. He's built his persona to touch upon those elements, but his work is grounded in a process of self-examination that feels very different. Kendrick's music does often remind me of what Stevie was doing with his major works of the early-to-mid 1970s. That kind of joy, complexity, and urgency."*
—ANN POWERS

months after I'd interned at the magazine; did he really deserve that coveted spot without a new album out? Increasingly, his very existence became hiphop's most must-watch reality show. Tupac shot it out with cops. His on-air interviews showed the brash bravura of Muhammad Ali. He survived five gunshots in a recording studio robbery. *Me Against the World* topped the *Billboard* chart while he sat in jail, for a sexual assault charge at a hotel my girlfriend once booked for her prom night. His beef with Biggie loomed larger, realer, than any rap beef we'd ever seen. The way he repped Death Row Records like a gang fascinated fans like me, without a real handle on what the consequences could be. No one expected another gunshot assault to kill him, he seemed invincible that way. His death gave the hiphop generation a taste of its own mortality. "Can't stop, won't stop" goes the credo . . . yet sometimes, we are stopped.

Kendrick Lamar prioritizes pro-blackness, spirituality, gangster tropes, and positivity in his art in ways obviously inspired by Tupac Shakur, but these two Geminis just as obviously look at life through alike eyes. Others have believed in the redemptive power of hiphop to save lives, many through personal experience. In the '70s, Afrika Bambaataa turned South Bronx gangs away from rivalries and violence with his Universal Zulu Nation organization, devoted to celebrating deejaying, emceeing, breakdancing, and aerosol art under one heading: hiphop. Hustlers, gangbangers, drug dealers, and exotic dancers (no dis to exotic dancers)—from Ice-T and Eazy-E to Cardi B and ScHoolboy Q—have all transformed themselves by turning toward rap and away from illegal shadow economies. KRS-One once ratified a Hiphop Declaration of Peace at the United Nations in 2001, in the hopes that positive principles for hiphop culture could be codified and followed. His approach, and the Temple of Hiphop he founded to achieve those ends, had its own problems, but he thought it was possible.

"I'm not saying I'm gonna change the world," Tupac once famously said, "but I guarantee that I will spark the brain that will change the world." He never saw himself as the type of change agent Malcolm X or even Obama was to African-American history. His aim was to inspire. I've seen Tupac T-shirts in the store windows of Paris, London, and Amsterdam, on the bodies of the young citizens of Algiers, Lagos, Berlin, and Guadalajara. Assailants murdered Biggie Smalls six months after Tupac, but his image isn't as ubiquitous. Pac has become a hiphop Che Guevara, a rap revolutionary. His unapologetic swagger and the black nationalism ideology he translated from his parents' Black Panther background to his hiphop audience make him one of the twentieth century's greatest musical legends. K-Dot went through Jay-Z and Lil Wayne phases searching for his own voice; but transcending to the level of rap revolutionary was an even loftier goal than the impossibility of rhyming like Jay.

Do rap's obsessives put Kendrick Lamar on the high-exalted pedestal of Tupac Shakur? No, not yet. Ironically, critics like dream hampton and Marc Lamont Hill (and this critic included) don't even consider Tupac to have been that fantastic of a rapper. In his lifetime, his Hollywood potential as a young, black Marlon Brando—in films like *Juice* and *Gridlock'd*—always impressed me more than his microphone skills. Based on pure rhyming ability, yes, technical rap aptitude weighs in Kendrick's favor. The passion that Pac puts behind his lines is also equally evident in Kendrick's material, from *Section.80* to *Black Panther: The Album*. "Alright" as a Movement for Black Lives anthem goes a long way in proving the transcendent power of Kendrick's music. The main reason why the spirit of Tupac Shakur lives in the DNA of Kendrick Lamar boils down to their influence outside of beats and rhymes.

Nipsey Hussle embodied the type of visionary activism and community philanthropy we might have expected from Kendrick by this point, given his deification of Tupac over the years. Before his murder in March 2019, the South Los Angeles rapper launched Vector90, a STEM center and coworking space in his local Crenshaw neighborhood. Laying down a blueprint for entrepreneurialism in the community, he'd funded improvements to urban L.A. schools, and died the day before a scheduled meeting with L.A.P.D. officials to prevent future gang violence. The long game of Kendrick Lamar's career has got to incorporate more grassroots, hands-on engagement in order to live up to the leadership expected of Tupac Shakur had he lived.

With *Illmatic*, hiphop showered a twenty-year-old Nas with unlimited praise for his debut album, not the least of which was calling the Queensbridge MC the next Rakim. Because since the mid-1980s, Rakim marked the Big Bang of all the polysyllabic, metaphysical rap flows to follow. Under the influence of jazz saxophonist's John Coltrane's melodic sheets of sound, Rakim's internal rhyme patterns, smooth yet stone-cold delivery, and more abstract, conceptual lyrics changed the culture forever. In the 1990s, Nas resurrected that attention to detail, that laser focus on complex, poetic wordplay, causing fans to regard him as Rakim's second coming. Despite all his other accolades and critical love, Kendrick has never been considered the Now incarnation of Nas, Biggie, Jay-Z, or any other hyper-lyrical MC. Yet there is no Kendrick without them, or Kool Moe Dee, Melle Mel, Rakim, Ice Cube, or any number of others.

So is he some sort of sum total of the rappers who've come before him? Exactly how much does Kendrick owe to the MCs who predate him? If his debt to Marvin Gaye, James Brown, and Tupac Shakur reveals a bit about where he stands in the

continuum of African-American culture, what unique thing does Kendrick bring to the table of black arts that hasn't been seen before?

As a teenager, I knew many an aspiring rapper. Hiphop represented a gold rush to a lot of us then, a fast track to fame and fortune at a young age. If LL Cool J or Roxanne Shanté could make it, why not try? And so they did. The first friend I ever made on my new college campus was a lacrosse player from Wyandanch, a suburban hamlet of Long Island, New York, where Rakim grew up. He went by the name Sahpreem, under the same Five Percent Nation sway that rechristened William Michael Griffin Jr. as the legendary Rakim. The thing about Sahpreem as an aspiring MC is that, to the trained ear, his flow and cadences were recognizable right away from popular rap songs of the day. He didn't steal rhymes; he used existing bar structures to guide his own rhymes. I knew a lot of high school rappers doing the same thing on the journey to discovering how to become the rappers they idolized. Still. Students who weren't homeboys with Sahpreem heard karaoke.

Wannabe MCs out to emulate the successful rappers of their day focus on their flows and cadences. They focus on their bar structures, subject matter, and overall lyricism. Voice is a factor: raising or lowering it, staying monotone, distorting it, processing it. They dedicate themselves to battle rhymes or introspective lines or gangster tropes or conscious platitudes or sex rhymes. In his arsenal, Kendrick Lamar uses all of the above. To compete with Kendrick, you're going to have to do *everything*. In this sense, he's the sum total of the microphone fiends who've come before him. His range from the pro-black "The Blacker the Berry" to the sentimental "For the Girlfriends" to the bars-bars-bars "Rigamortis" to the spiritual "Faith"—and Kendrick's overachieving consistence of skill throughout that range—gives him the distinctive stamp that artists who stand on his shoulders will need to replicate one day.

# m.A.A.d city

To paraphrase the 2004 anthology *Lit Riffs: Writers "Cover" Songs They Love*, I always thought rap songs were short stories, only better. Believing that hip-hop occasionally approaches the level of high literature has the same connotation as expressing that African Americans are so articulate and well-spoken. Why wouldn't the best of a genre based so heavily on the power of words produce works equal to Colson Whitehead, Chimamanda Ngozi Adichie, John Edgar Wideman, or any other great novelist?

Five years before my own Kendrick Lamar course at NYU, English professor Adam Diehl at Georgia Regents University taught *good kid, m.A.A.d city* alongside James Joyce's classic autobiographical novel, *A Portrait of the Artist as a Young Man*. One of Kendrick's greatest strengths as a lyricist is his world-building ability to lace his rhymes with all the details, plot twists, and gravitas one would expect from a master storyteller from literature or cinema.

Writing a short story that takes all of its cues from Kendrick Lamar's *good kid, m.A.A.d city* story line would be the plainest way to demonstrate the literary value of his work. He should be considered equally as much of a poet, writer, or author as he is a rap artist, and literally adapting his full-length album into literature would provide all the proof anyone needs. But turning his preexisting artistic statement into my own self-contained "m.A.A.d city" story takes us into the murky legal waters of derivative works. Still, when properly examined, it becomes clear that Lamar's first major classic is already a *New Yorker*–worthy short story in its own fashion.

# m.A.A.d city

### Miles Marshall Lewis
(after Kendrick Lamar)

# Chronology

The out-of-sequence narrative Kendrick confronts listeners with on *good kid, m.A.A.d city* is the first thing to deal with in disentangling his story line and making it easier to follow. Critics elevated Quentin Tarantino's *Pulp Fiction* to a genius level partially because of its structure, a nonlinear unfolding of three interrelated sequences that ultimately influenced our homegrown hero from Compton when recording his breakthrough. However, "Sherane a.k.a Master Splinter's Daughter" appears as song number one on the album, and accurately enough, it is actually where Kendrick's tale begins.

The track sets up Sherane as the love interest of *good kid, m.A.A.d city*, the center of tragedies that develop several songs later. As a prelude to the main story line, Kendrick uses this opener to sketch out his femme fatale and explain how they first met. Color is key when it comes to painting pictures for readers (or listeners) to fill in with their minds' eye, something Kendrick clearly understands. Beginning the short story with "Sherane a.k.a Master Splinter's Daughter" goes easiest by using the details already there.

Sherane meets our protagonist at a Compton house party, on El Segundo Boulevard and South Central Avenue. According to our reliable narrator, the teenager's shapely figure recalls exotic dancers from the famed strip clubs of Atlanta, and music by Ciara rocks the living room dance floor. (In a deeper dive, Kendrick confirms on the Genius website that the specific song in question is "1, 2 Step," her 2004 banger featuring Missy Elliott.) Kendrick divides the song into two parts: their initial meeting and a time much later when he heads to her house for, hopefully, sex. To hold his story in our minds in its proper order, we'll have to shuffle their booty call to later on. Scene one consists of young Kenny Duckworth sipping cognac liqueur from one of those ubiquitous red SOLO cups, flirting with a sexy girl from the wrong side of town (Paramount, he rhymes) while his homeboys hold the wall. He's already mentally recasting her in the Kama Sutra before he even leaves the party; he scores the the number of her Nextel and jets.

On "Sherane a.k.a Master Splinter's Daughter," Kendrick makes it clear that a summer passes before the Compton house party and his attempt to seal the deal sexually. The song reveals a lot about Sherane, details that can be written out as the two getting to know each other over pre-iPhone text messages: she lives in Paramount with a grandma and two brothers; her mother struggled with crack cocaine; her gangster cousin Demetrius is not to be trifled with. The specifics are all there in Kendrick's lyrics ("Her mother was a crack addict/She live with her granny and her younger two brothers/Her favorite cousin Demetrius is irrepetible . . ."). Locating the star-crossed lovers in their respective bedrooms texting on dumbphones, the reader is placed right there underneath the streetlight streaming onto Kendrick's mattress from his window, as they formulate hookup plans straight from details elsewhere on *good kid, m.A.A.d city*: hijacking his mother's purple Dodge Caravan from her place after a game of basketball with his boys in Gonzales Park, for example. Imagine some sexy playfulness from Sherane's direction—proof of her allure, evidence for Kenny's attraction to her—and we're onto the next song.

"Backseat Freestyle" comes up two tracks later; we'll need to skip "Bitch, Don't Kill My Vibe" to maintain the flow of the narrative. As its title suggests, Kendrick Duckworth dives into full K-Dot mode from the backseat of a friend's Toyota, freestyling bars about "the mind state of being sixteen years old and not having no cares in the world," Kendrick has said. A skit preceding "Backseat Freestyle" sets the scenario of Kenny's posse egging him on to rhyme over a beat CD spinning in the car stereo.

Act one of the *good kid, m.A.A.d city* drama truly begins on the next track, "The Art of Peer Pressure." The inciting incident of the album's whole redemption story line starts with the home invasion robbery perpetrated by Kenny and his boys, who subsequently engage in a high-speed escape from the L.A.P.D. The song's mention of "basketball shorts with the Gonzales Park odor" places this section of the story at Gonzales Park, at the close of a four-man game that ends in talk about Kenny's plans for the evening ("I know he tryna fuck on Sherane tonight") taken straight from the skit.

"The Art of Peer Pressure" marks the point when Kenny smokes his first and last joint of marijuana, discovering soon that one of his homies laced it with angel dust. The verses are ripe for literary illustration. In the song, the party of four drive by some sex workers. Given the tales on *Section.80*, maybe they're cruising the same stretch of Long Beach Boulevard immortalized on "Keisha's Song (Her Pain)." Next stop: Westchester High ("We speedin' on the 405, passin' Westchester . . ."). Flirting with a bourgeois female student body quickly shifts into an unnecessary fistfight with a Crip on the school grounds. Kenny and his posse jump him, hop back in the Toyota, and speed off, laughing.

*"I think Kendrick is just a really strong writer. He has this incredible ability to zero in on the smallest characteristics and use them to say so much. For me, the pinnacle of this is 'The Art of Peer Pressure' (echoes of [Slick Rick's]* The Art of Storytelling*), where he paints this kid who's living the life but knows in his heart he isn't about that life. And Kendrick conveys that with all of these small, knowing nods. My personal fave is that brief line, 'look at me—I got the blunt in my mouth.' The 'look at me' gives us a glimpse into the insecurity he feels, and I guess more importantly, the vulnerability."*

—TA-NEHISI COATES

Finally, the foursome arrive at a house they've been staking out for the past two months. As they break in and commence robbing the place, perhaps this scene marks the beginning of Kendrick Duckworth's bad trip. The hallucinogenic effect of his sherm stick could affect his perception of the living room, kitchen, and backyard, their getting caught raiding the house, their quick-fast evacuation and narrow escape after getting chased by the cops. Like Hemingway or Slick Rick, Kendrick provides a plethora of details to play with: a Young Jeezy CD playing in the car, a homeboy's pack of Black & Mild cigarillos, etc. A skit at the end cues listeners into the post-robbery conversation between the crew, as they deal with Kenny's angel dust high and hatch plans for the nighttime.

Things get *Pulp Fiction* wonky here chronologically. As "The Art of Peer Pressure" (track number four) concludes, Kenny gets dropped off at home by his crew to detox for his meet-up with Sherane that night. But at the end of "Compton" (track number twelve) concluding the album, Kenny asks his mom to borrow her Caravan for fifteen minutes. Like a narrative Möbius strip, this leads us back to the beginning of the album, which starts with his mother's answering machine message demanding the return of the Caravan that he didn't ask to borrow until the end of *good kid, m.A.A.d city.* Or was her voicemail some kind of foreshadowing?

228

Hold this timetable in mind: the skit that concludes "Compton" leads back to the first half of "Sherane a.k.a Master Splinter's Daughter," then the skit that ends "Bitch, Don't Kill My Vibe," "Backseat Freestyle," and "The Art of Peer Pressure." That's so far; back to the story.

Kendrick Duckworth has gotten himself together, sleeping off the laced blunt and vowing never to get high again. Chronologically, we're back to the second half of "Sherane a.k.a Master Splinter's Daughter"—where he rhymes about being stuck in traffic behind a Corvette, low on gas and on his way to see Sherane. Let's conjecture a bit when it comes to Kendrick's inner monologue after coming a hair's breadth away from catching his first felony charge, and maybe even just as close to some sort of overdose. We've reached the point in the album's plot somewhere between the end of "Sherane a.k.a Master Splinter's Daughter" ("I pulled up, a smile on my face, and then I see/Two niggas, two black hoodies . . .") and track eight, "m.A.A.d city" ("Fuck who you know—where you from, my nigga?").

*"I would argue that poetry aspires to hiphop. Hiphop is most powerful when it is aware of its vibration and cool. It reaches people. Great poetry confronts, disrupts, and alters our sense of self, but hiphop is also a vibe. Poetry is best when it is concerned with truth-telling and meaning. Hiphop is an act of self-determination and the greatest hiphop moments are rooted in a poetic awareness. We can't separate hiphop and poetry. There is poetry in our music, our dance, our fight, our survival, our turn-up, our escapism, and our love. Poetry is not limited to the realm of words. We communicate and demonstrate our values through our creative expression. Hiphop is the black spirit in action. It's a meditation between music and words. Our experience here together in America informs how and why we create the way we do. If capitalism rewarded truth-telling, we would have a very different relationship to hiphop. Hiphop was born in the nitty-gritty reality of exploitation for profit and originally sought to create an alternative reality where we could tell our stories and honor our depth even in our party and bullshit. Hiphop became commodified and it lost its sense of poetry in the process."*

—AJA MONET

By the conclusion of "m.A.A.d city," Kenny's crew consoles him in a skit after his critical beatdown. His assault marks the beginning of the album's act two. Ordering the songs in a proper time arrangement means going back to track five, "Money Trees," where he mentions events ("Home invasion was persuasive . . ." "I fucked Sherane and went to tell my bros . . .") that have happened by the time he's licking wounds with his posse later on. "Swimming Pools (Drank)" follows "m.A.A.d city" on the record and within the plot of *good kid, m.A.A.d city*. Given the alcoholic theme of the song, we can imagine Kenny drinking with his crew to ease the pain. The outro to the song takes us right back amongst them, cruising for revenge. Shots are fired; a character named Dave dies ("These bitch-ass niggas killed my brother!" yells out another character), and the turning point to the album arrives. K-Dot evolves into Kendrick Lamar, renewing himself spiritually on "Sing About Me, I'm Dying of Thirst" and fully dedicating himself to an artistic path. The album-closing "Compton," featuring Dr. Dre, serves as a celebration of Kendrick Lamar as the great rapper ready to take on the world that he's become.

A reorganized timeline of the record looks like this:

**230**

"Compton" (skit)

"Sherane a.k.a Master Splinter's Daughter"

"Bitch, Don't Kill My Vibe" (skit)

"Backseat Freestyle"

"The Art of Peer Pressure"

"Compton" (skit) again

"Sherane a.k.a Master Splinter's Daughter" again

"Poetic Justice"

"good kid"

"m.A.A.d city"

"Money Trees"

"Sing About Me, I'm Dying of Thirst"

"Real"

"Compton" (skit) again

# Characters

In 2011, the Roots released an album called *undun*—an existential concept album wherein the songs related the album's story in a reverse-chronological order, and all of rapper Black Thought's rhymes were told from the first-person perspective of a character named Redford Stevens. Going back further to 1999, producer-rapper Prince Paul dropped his second studio album, *A Prince Among Thieves*—another concept record wherein rapper Breezly Brewin' assumes the character of Tariq, a wannabe MC who enters a life of crime trying to raise funds to record a demo. I raise these examples to underline that the main character of *good kid, m.A.A.d city* needn't be assumed to be Kendrick Lamar. In evaluating *good kid, m.A.A.d city* as the short story it clearly is, another first step is getting a handle on the characters as presented.

Kendrick does indeed introduce himself to Sherane by his government name ("My name is Kendrick") on "Sherane a.k.a Master Splinter's Daughter." This Kendrick lives with his parents in Compton and spends time with a posse of high school homies who shoot basketball, drink, smoke, and occasionally hatch illegal schemes. An aspiring teenage rapper, he's torn between a hood life of suspect choices that his friends also navigate daily and dreams of a prosperous rap career. Sex with Sherane also tops his list of motivations, but what makes Kendrick tick is overcoming peer pressure and the pull of his neighborhood's criminal temptations to make a positive impact on Compton as a homegrown superstar artist. Art imitates life imitates art.

Without Sherane, nothing gets set in motion for Kendrick to eventually be redeemed, permanently set on the path to become true to himself. She's nevertheless sort of a cipher. We know Kendrick's attracted to her body, which reminds him of a stripper's. (In the visuals for "Backseat Freestyle," curvy model Asia Walker portrays Sherane twerking in her panties next to a luxury car.) She seems interested in him, but we're never quite sure why—or even if—she set him up to get jumped by gang-bangers in "m.A.A.d city." Listeners with a literary eye might need to infer a motivation for Sherane, maybe something to do with her disdain over discovering the

*"Tupac was an era and Kendrick Lamar is his own era. He speaks to a time and place in our generation that Tupac doesn't. Every generation demands a new voice and is seeking its autonomy. Tupac forever changed our relationship to lyricism, voice, content, and artistic responsibility. I can't speak for Kendrick Lamar's political education, but it is very clear that Tupac saw himself as a voice of the people; he was well read and politicized by a movement for black liberation. Afeni Shakur has everything to do with Tupac's relationship to literacy, this country, and ultimately his philosophy on life. We cannot tell the story about Tupac without speaking about his mother and the conditions she was forced to raise him in. His life was a poem. Kendrick Lamar may not have been raised by a Black Panther, but he is deeply aware of how the personal is political. I think this is the heart of what makes fans gravitate towards both poets. Kendrick Lamar could not exist without Tupac, but his greatness will be determined by how he evolves the conversation between lyricist and listener. In the same vein as Tupac, Kendrick has disrupted pop culture with grassroots truth-telling. He's found a way to morph into characters and to use music in a way that gets young people to care about the lyrics. Both artists are street poets and they aspire to lyrical greatness. They use metaphors to decolonize black consciousness."*

—AJA MONET

nickname "Master Splinter's daughter" and exacting revenge for the subtle dis.

Rounding out *good kid, m.A.A.d city*'s main cast of characters are Kendrick's crew. He names them all at once on "m.a.a.d city" ("It was me, L Boog, and Yan Yan, YG Lucky ride down Rosecrans . . ." ). According to "The Art of Peer Pressure," one of them owns a Toyota and another owns a firearm ("Me and my niggas four deep in a white Toyota/A quarter tank of gas, one pistol, and orange soda"). One of them is related to Dave, who's murdered in retaliation against the Crips who beat Kendrick up for visiting Sherane. Most of the album's dialogue comes from this band of brothers, and the voicemail messages of Kendrick's mom. For the sake of characterization, assigning one of them (let's say Yan Yan) a shady nature could prove effective.

By the time Kendrick struggles with his angel dust high, his sheisty companion would be the first to feign innocence, as per one of the album's skits:

"I think he hit the wrong blunt," YG Lucky says.

"Nah, that nigga straight. He ain't hit that one," Yan Yan lies.

# Dialogue

Having already sorted the *Tenet*-twisted chronology, we're aware that Kendrick's story begins at a house party on El Segundo and North Central Avenue. The first dialogue in the story to be drawn directly from the album is between Kendrick and Sherane when they meet. Setting the scene, the two slide bits of conversation in between dancing to Ciara under crimson party lights:

"My name is Kendrick."

"No . . . You're Handsome," says Sherane.

"Where you stay?"

"Down the street from Dominguez High,"

she says, cracking a wad of strawberry bubblegum.

"That's borderline Compton or Paramount. Well, is it Compton?"

"No."

And after a brief section calculating the math of gang territories and hood affiliations:

"What you tryna get into?"

"*[Vulnerability], that too sets Kendrick apart. Hiphop is built on rappers portraying themselves as invulnerable. Kendrick somehow managed to make hiphop with its own share of shit-talking that still confessed his own precarious position. It made his voice much more complex, and much more literary than usual.*"

—TA-NEHISI COATES

The language of their interchange comes right from "Sherane a.k.a Master Splinter's Daughter" and tells us all we need to know. Following up the house party with late-night sexting between the two in their respective bedrooms, the opportunity presents itself to use Kendrick's sprung admission from later in the song:

"I wanna come over, what's up?"

The skits of the album provide most of the story's dialogue: mostly banter between Kendrick and his boys and voicemail messages from his mother, Paula Oliver, along with an encounter with a neighborhood grandma (voiced by the late Maya Angelou on the album), reciting the Sinner's Prayer on the skit in between "Sing About Me, I'm Dying of Thirst" and "Real."

Either Yan Yan or L Boogie or YG Lucky chide Kendrick to get in the Toyota after their ball game at Gonzales Park, exhortations from the skit following "Bitch, Don't Kill My Vibe." The same voice pipes up telling him to prepare his freestyles for the ride down Interstate 405 to cruise the sex workers and, eventually, the moneyed girls over at Westchester High School— "on the mission for bad bitches and trouble." The next time someone speaks, the squad escapes police after their aborted home invasion and Kendrick is dealing with his dangerous dose of angel dust and Hennessy.

Listeners hear from Kendrick's mother a total of three times over the course of *good kid, m.A.A.d city*, each time through voicemail messages where she mainly pleads for the return of her Dodge Caravan. We hear from his father, Kenny Duckworth, at length only once, though his interjections interrupting his wife's messages make for great comic relief. In a short story, each of Paula Oliver's voicemails would be quoted standalone style and in full, beginning right after Kendrick spills his guts on the pavement above. (She also calls him during the burglary, which can be incorporated into the prose too.)

Quote one, Paula confronts Kendrick with his promise to return the van in just fifteen minutes, reminding him about closing hours at the county building where she receives the family's food stamps. His siblings are hungry, and she hopes that the Dodge isn't being used for anything involving "damn hoodrats out there . . . especially that crazy-ass girl, Sherane." She also reveals that Kendrick is on his way to eleventh grade, placing him at sixteen years old. For his part, papa Kenny Duckworth demands his misplaced dominos. Quote two, his mother says that she rescheduled her SNAP appointment. She now wants her Dodge back to have some alone time away from her husband, who's "feelin' good as a motherfucker . . . high as hell."

The final voicemail belongs to both of Kendrick's parents, after Kendrick and his boys recite

"*I use him, like I use other great MCs, for inspiration—to remember what I'm aspiring to as a writer. Hiphop is the first literature I remember. It was the first place I heard words and narrative used in a beautiful way. In some profound way, I'm always trying to recapture that amazing feeling I had when trying to memorize 'The Show' or 'Roxanne, Roxanne,' 'The Grand Finalé' or 'I Know You Got Soul.' Kendrick has all of that in him. And when I hear him, I feel it, and it's that same thing I'm trying to convey to a reader.*"
—TA-NEHISI COATES

**237**

the Sinner's Prayer at the Food 4 Less parking lot. Crips have already murdered Dave and Kendrick's dad expresses condolences. More than that, he doles out hard-won advice to his oldest son: "Any nigga can kill a man, that don't make you a real nigga. Real is responsibility. Real is taking care of your motherfuckin' family. Real is God, nigga." For her third and final quote, Paula says neighbors told her about Kendrick and his friends in the supermarket parking lot getting preached to, and "that's what y'all need."

*"There's so many [Kendrick songs] that are poems. 'These Walls' is layered and he's playing on the literal definition of walls and also on the metaphor of being inside a woman. I love 'u' because great poetry is deeply personal and also political. He talks about being at war with one's self. And there's also 'His Pain II,' which feels like a prayer and a poem. Kendrick has a way of making poetic anthems. He found a way to make poems into songs and to do it well because he goes deep into the reservoir of self and uncovers the music of meaning. He's not afraid to be vulnerable and yet he never isolates his listener; he speaks with us not at us."*

—AJA MONET

*"I think Kelefa Sanneh once wrote a piece arguing against hiphop as poetry—not because hiphop has no literary qualities, but because it implies that poetry is the thing hiphop should aspire to. And I kind of think it's the other way around—or at least that it can go both ways. So I don't know if I'd make the poetry comparison."*

—TA-NEHISI COATES

Paula's final words carry much of the moral weight of *good kid, m.A.A.d city*. She says that Top Dawg has called the house asking for him to show up to the recording studio with producer Dave Free, and encourages her son to take his creative ambitions seriously. "Mama Said Knock You Out," LL Cool J's 1991 single, might have been the most encouraging words ever heard in hiphop from mother to son until Paula's outro on *good kid, m.A.A.d city*: "If I don't hear from you by tomorrow, I hope you come back and learn from your mistakes. Come back a man, tell your story to these black and brown kids in Compton. Let 'em know you was just like them, but you still rose from that dark place of violence, becoming a positive person. But when you do make it, give back with your words of encouragement. That's the best way to give back to your city. And I love you, Kendrick . . ."

And so perhaps Kendrick Lamar in the *New Yorker* would end a stylized short story version of the album on the same triumphant note as the closing track of "Compton," something like this conclusion here:

Kendrick Lamar pops sugared flakes of Fruity Pebbles cereal into his mouth, rolling down Rosecrans Avenue on a bright Saturday morning headed to Carson, full of ideas. All kinds of designs come to him all the time now, ever since the funerals of Dave and his brother, Marcus, weeks

**240**

ago (R.I.P. YG Lucky). Thinking big is his new normal. He wants to record an album focused on the after-effects of the 1980s on his generation. He wants to make another album following a day in the life of a good kid in the mad city of the Compton hood. Narratives could be told out of chronological order; characters in his raps could bleed from one album to the next, Easter eggs for his most devoted fans. He'll have fans, he's sure of it. DJ Dave Free, Top Dawg, the rest of the homies at Top's house, they've seen the change since he buried K-Dot and decided to present himself as himself: Kendrick Lamar. The OG Keith Murray did it. Kanye West, of course, Talib Kweli, Nas. The change in identity opened up new possibilities for his voice, the things he wants to say to the world. He's not going to be only speaking to his neighborhood, not only, that's not the goal anymore. Maybe you can't take the hood out of the boy, but he sees hiphop taking the boy out of the hood. Way out. Flying him far away from the four corners of 137th Street. Watch that black boy fly, he thinks.

# Kendrick Chorus

**Dart Adams** is a Bostonian historian, music journalist, and lecturer. He's previously written for Okayplayer, *Mass Appeal*, *Complex*, NPR, and *Ebony*. Adams is also owner/operator of Producers I Know/Fat Beats and hosts two podcasts, Dart Against Humanity and The Boston Legends.

**Ivie Ani** is a Nigerian-American multimedia journalist and writer covering culture. A native New Yorker and NYU alumna, her writing has been published in *The New York Times*, *Vanity Fair*, *The Village Voice*, *Teen Vogue*, *Paper*, *Complex*, Okayplayer, OkayAfrica, *Grazia* UK, and NYU's *Social and Cultural Analysis* journal. Ani has spoken at Harvard University, New York University, and Wesleyan University, and has done on-air commentary for BBC Radio, BET, *Entertainment Tonight*, Fox 5 NY, Genius, Hot 97, and more.

**Kevin L. Clark** is a Brooklyn-based journalist, screenwriter, and health advocate. A native of Akron, Ohio, his writing has been published in *Ebony*, *Black Enterprise*, *XXL*, *Vibe*, *Complex*, and Okayplayer, where he served as the site's managing editor. Clark is also a recent kidney transplant recipient, using his second chance to develop a comedy TV show exploring health-care issues that affect the black and brown community.

**Ta-Nehisi Coates** is the author of *The Beautiful Struggle*, *We Were Eight Years in Power*, *The Water Dancer*, and *Between the World and Me*, which won the National Book Award in 2015. He is a recipient of a MacArthur Fellowship.

**kris ex** is a Los Angeles–based music critic published in *Rolling Stone*, *Billboard*, Pitchfork, and many other magazines and websites. He's also co-author of the *New York Times* bestselling 50 Cent memoir *From Pieces to Weight: Once Upon a Time in Southside Queens* and the 1999 Pras Michel novel, *Ghetto Supastar*.

**Alicia Garza** is a co-founder of Black Lives Matter. She is currently an Oakland-based organizer, writer, and public speaker serving as the Strategy and Partnerships Director for the National Domestic Workers' Alliance. A contributing editor for *Marie Claire*, she is also working on a new initiative called the Black Future's Lab. Garza released *The Purpose of Power: How We Come Together When We Fall Apart* in 2020.

**Farah Jasmine Griffin** is chair of the African-American and African Diaspora Studies department at Columbia University. She is the author of several books, including *Who Set You Flowin?: The African-American Migration Narrative, Beloved Sisters and Loving Friends: Letters from Rebecca Primus of Royal Oak, Maryland, and Addie Brown of Hartford, Connecticut, 1854–1868*, and *If You Can't Be Free, Be a Mystery: In Search of Billie Holiday*. Griffin sat on the committee that nominated Kendrick Lamar for the 2018 Pulitzer Prize for Music.

**William E. Ketchum III** is a journalist with fifteen years of experience covering music, TV/film, pop culture, race, mental health, and social justice. His writings and commentary have been featured in *Billboard*, *Complex*, Okayplayer, *The Guardian*, NPR, MTV, BBC, and more. He also served as the deputy editor of *Vibe*.

**Jason King** is Associate Professor, Director of Global Studies, and Director of Writing, History & Emergent Media Studies, and the founding faculty member at New York University's Clive Davis Institute of Recorded Music. He is the curator of Future Pop Music Studies, an exploratory NYU study abroad program based in Berlin. A journalist, musician, DJ, and producer, he is a regular contributor to publications like Pitchfork, NPR, *Billboard*, Red Bull Music Academy, Buzzfeed, and Slate and is the author of *The Michael Jackson Treasures*, a 2009 Barnes & Noble exclusive biography on the King of Pop.

**Aja Monet** is a Caribbean-American poet. Her poems are wise, lyrical, and courageous. In 2007, Monet won the legendary Nuyorican Poets Café Grand Slam title at nineteen and has been internationally recognized for combining her spellbound voice and vivid poetic imagery on stage. Monet's first full collection of poetry, *My Mother Was a Freedom Fighter*, was nominated for an NAACP Image Award for Outstanding Literary Work.

**Darnell L. Moore** is head of strategy and programs at Breakthrough U.S. He is the author of the 2019 Lambda Literary Award–winning memoir, *No Ashes in the Fire: Coming of Age Black & Free in America*, a 2018 New York Times Notable Book and Barnes & Noble Discover Great New Readers pick. In addition, he is co-managing editor at The Feminist Wire and an editor of The Feminist Wire Books. Moore is also a writer-in-residence at the Center on African-American Religion, Sexual Politics, and Social Justice at Columbia University.

**Ann Powers** is a critic and correspondent for NPR Music. She is the author of several books, most recently *Good Booty: Love and Sex, Black and White, Body and Soul in American Music*. She lives in Nashville and is currently working on a critical biography of Joni Mitchell.

**Jay Smooth** is the founder of New York's longest-running hiphop radio show, The Underground Railroad, which aired for more than twenty-five years on WBAI radio and now broadcasts independently at Hiphopmusic.com. Smooth is also acclaimed for his cultural commentary on the Ill Doctrine video blog, where his takes on politics and culture have been hailed by political commentator Rachel Maddow as "genius," and cited by Chuck D as home to "the best hiphop conversations."

**Greg Tate** is a writer, musician, and cultural provocateur who lives in Harlem. His books include *Flyboy in the Buttermilk*, *Flyboy 2: The Greg Tate Reader*, *Midnight Lightning: Jimi Hendrix and the Black Experience*, and *Everything But the Burden: What White People Are Taking from Black Culture*. Since 1999, he has led the conducted improv big band, Burnt Sugar the Arkestra Chamber.

# Acknowledgments

As I write these bons mots of gratitude, I'm also halfway finished editing my mom's second novel—her latest retirement project that's proven once again where the genes of my creativity come from. An eternal thank-you then to my mother, Brenda Joyner: for her Pollyanna positivity, her Lucy Ricardo–like bright ideas, her endless maternal patience, and love. Thanks, too, for the toy typewriters and tape recorders. (They came in handy.)

For taking me to comic conventions, introducing me to James Brown and Miles Davis—for schooling me on black Woodstock, Four Tops vs. Temptations choreography, the cute drummer in *Beyond the Valley of the Dolls*, 007's cocktail cuffs, Sly's wedding at Madison Square Garden, Jagger's twenty-ninth birthday party at the St. Regis, and countless more mental memorabilia—I thank my father, Darryl Lewis. I owe my attentive ears to you. (Sorry about your suede boots.)

To my agent, Tanya McKinnon, and her indefatigable editorial director, Carol Taylor, a major, major thanks. To editrix Kierna Mayo, who first set me up with Kendrick Lamar in sunny California for the interview that set all this off, you know what it is: thanks for believing in the right place at the right time. And for the tireless work of my bawse editor, Monique Patterson, and all hands on deck at St. Martin's Press, another major thanks. #TrustBlackWomen is a hashtag for a reason.

When people know all about you but like you anyway, that's friendship. For all the bottomless wine and good times, special thanks to Aleijuan Afuraka, Alexandra Phanor-Faury, Angelique Hancock, Charmaine Delatour, Dimitry Elias Léger, Elsa Mehary, Michael A. Gonzales, Ron Worthy, and my blood brothers, Chris and Kyle Lewis. With at least two ride or dies in your lifetime, you're lucky. I've got at least ten.

Thanks to the Clive Davis Institute of Recorded Music, and the goody-goodies of my 2019 Kendrick class: Jessica Howard, Gabi Grella, Matt Lacey, and Ethan Zingalis, continued success to you geniuses. Shout-out to Datwon Thomas for showing up as guest speaker with unwavering, contagious love for hiphop.

And everlasting thanks to my *choubidou chouchou* of a partner, Christine Herelle-Lewis. *Je t'aime.*

# DISCOGRAPHY

## KENDRICK LAMAR ALBUM RELEASES

### Section.80 (2011)
Top Dawg

**Released:** July 2, 2011
**Producers:** Sounwave, Terrace Martin, J.Cole, Wyldfyer, Tommy Black, Dave Free, Tae Beast, THC, Willie B
**Featured artists:** Ab-Soul ("Ab-Soul's Outro"), BJ the Chicago Kid ("Kush & Corinthians (His Pain)"), Colin Munroe ("No Make-Up (Her Vice)"), GLC ("Poe Mans Dreams (His Vice)"), ScHoolboy Q ("The Spiteful Chant"), Ash Riser ("Keisha's Song (Her Pain)"), RZA ("Ronald Reagan Era")

**Tracks:**
1. "F*ck Your Ethnicity"
2. "Hol' Up"
3. "A.D.H.D."
4. "No Make-Up (Her Vice)"
5. "Tammy's Song (Her Evils)"
6. "Chapter Six"
7. "Ronald Reagan Era (His Evils)"
8. "Poe Mans Dreams (His Vice)"
9. "The Spiteful Chant"
10. "Chapter Ten"
11. "Keisha's Song (Her Pain)"
12. "Rigamortis"
13. "Kush & Corinthians (His Pain)"
14. "Blow My High (Members Only)"
15. "Ab-Soul's Outro"
16. "HiiiPoWeR"

### good kid, m.A.A.d city (2012)
Top Dawg/Aftermath/Interscope

**Released:** October 22, 2012
**Producers:** Jack Splash, Hit-Boy, Like, Scoop DeVille, DJ Dahi, Skhye Hutch, Just Blaze, Tha Bizness, T-Minus, Pharrell Williams, Rahki, Terrace Martin, THC, Sounwave
**Featured artists:** Dr. Dre ("Compton"), Drake ("Poetic Justice"), MC Eiht ("m.A.A.d City"), Jay Rock ("Money Trees"), Anna Wise ("Real")

**Tracks:**
1. "Sherane a.k.a. Master Splinter's Daughter"
2. "Bitch, Don't Kill My Vibe"
3. "Backseat Freestyle"
4. "The Art of Peer Pressure"
5. "Money Trees"
6. "Poetic Justice"
7. "good kid"
8. "m.A.A.d city"
9. "Swimming Pools (Drank)"
10. "Sing About Me, I'm Dying of Thirst"
11. "Real"
12. "Compton"

### To Pimp a Butterfly (2015)
Top Dawg/Aftermath/Interscope

**Released:** March 16, 2015
**Producers:** Flying Lotus, Ronald "Flippa" Colson, Sounwave, Terrace Martin, Rahki, Tommy Black, Larrance Dopson, Taz Arnold, Thundercat, Whoarei, Pharrell Williams, Knxwledge, Tae Beast, LoveDragon, Boi-1da, Koz
**Featured artists:** George Clinton ("Wesley's Theory"), Thundercat ("Wesley's Theory," "Institutionalized," "These Walls"), Bilal ("Institution-

alized," "These Walls"), Anna Wise ("Institution-alized"), Snoop Dogg ("Institutionalized"), James Fauntleroy ("How Much a Dollar Cost"), Ronald Isley ("How Much a Dollar Cost"), Rapsody ("Complexion (A Zulu Love)")

**Tracks:**
1. "Wesley's Theory"
2. "For Free? (Interlude)"
3. "King Kunta"
4. "Institutionalized"
5. "These Walls"
6. "u"
7. "Alright"
8. "For Sale? (Interlude)"
9. "Momma"
10. "Hood Politics"
11. "How Much a Dollar Cost"
12. "Complexion (A Zulu Love)"
13. "The Blacker the Berry"
14. "You Ain't Gotta Lie (Momma Said)"
15. "i"
16. "Mortal Man"

## untitled unmastered (2016)
Top Dawg/Aftermath/Interscope

**Released:** March 4, 2016
**Producers:** Astronote, Cardo, Egypt, Frank Dukes, Terrace Martin, Mono/Poly, Ali Sha-heed Muhammad, Ritz Reynolds, Sounwave, Thundercat, Swizz Beatz, Adrian Younge, Yung Exclusive
**Featured artists:** Bilal ("untitled 01 | 08.19.2014.," "untitled 03 | 05.28.2013.," "untitled 05 | 09.21.2014."), Anna Wise ("untitled 01 | 08.19.2014.," "untitled 05 | 09.21.2014."), Mani Strings ("untitled 03 | 05.28.2013."), Rocket

("untitled 04 | 08.14.2014."), SZA ("untitled 04 | 08.14.2014.," "untitled 05 | 09.21.2014.," "un-titled 07 | 2014 - 2016"), Punch ("untitled 05 | 09.21.2014."), Jay Rock ("untitled 05 | 09.21.2014."), Cee Lo ("untitled 06 | 06.30.2014."), Egypt ("unti-tled 07 | 2014 - 2016"), Thundercat ("untitled 08 | 09.06.2014.")

**Tracks:**
1. "untitled 01 | 08.19.2014."
2. "untitled 02 | 06.23.2014."
3. "untitled 03 | 05.28.2013."
4. "untitled 04 | 08.14.2014."
5. "untitled 05 | 09.21.2014."
6. "untitled 06 | 06.30.2014."
7. "untitled 07 | 2014 - 2016"
8. "untitled 08 | 09.06.2014."

## DAMN. (2017)
Top Dawg/Aftermath/Interscope

**Released:** April 14, 2017
**Producers:** 9th Wonder, The Alchemist, BAD-BADNOTGOOD, Bekon, Cardo, DJ Dahi, Greg Kurstin, James Blake, Mike WiLL Made-It, Ricci Riera, Sounwave, Steve Lacy, Terrace Martin, Teddy Walton, Top Dawg
**Featured artists:** Rihanna ("LOYALTY."), Zacari ("LOVE."), U2 ("XXX.")

**Tracks:**
1. "BLOOD."
2. "DNA."
3. "YAH."
4. "ELEMENT."
5. "FEEL."
6. "LOYALTY."
7. "PRIDE."

**8.** "HUMBLE."
**9.** "LUST."
**10.** "LOVE."
**11.** "XXX."
**12.** "FEAR."
**13.** "GOD."
**14.** "DUCKWORTH."

## KENDRICK LAMAR MIXTAPE RELEASES

### Y.H.N.I.C. (Hub City Threat: Minor of the Year) (2004)
Konkrete Jungle Muzik

**Released:** 2004
**Producers:** 100 Miles And Runnin', Dr. Dre, Just Blaze, K-Rob, Mannie Fresh, Mike Elizondo, The Neptunes, Scram Jones
**Featured artists:** Dave Free ("Go DJ," "Drop It Like It's Hot (Freestyle)"), Freeway ("Ride Up"), Joe Budden ("Ride Up")

Tracks:
**1.** "Intro (Hova Song Freestyle)"
**2.** "What the Deal"
**3.** "Compton Life"
**4.** "Go DJ"
**5.** "Hovi Baby"
**6.** "Put That on Something"
**7.** "Ride Up"
**8.** "How We Do"
**9.** "Drop It Like It's Hot (Freestyle)"
**10.** "Industry Niggas (Skit)"
**11.** "Biggie"

### Training Day (2005)
Top Dawg

**Released:** December 20, 2005
**Producers:** DJ Khalil, DJ Skee, Dr. Dre, J Dilla, Jon Brion, Kanye West, Mark Batson, Nashiem Myrick, THC
**Featured artists:** Punch ("Blow Them Horns," "J Dilla (Freestyle)," "Prototype," "Dreams," "Imagine"), Jay Rock ("Gz and Hustlas," "J Dilla (Freestyle)," "Imagine"), Emjae ("Get Throwed"), Dave Free ("Interview with DJ Dave Part 3," "Interview with DJ Dave Part 4," "Interview with DJ Dave Part 5")

Tracks:
**1.** "One Shot Kill"
**2.** "Blame God"
**3.** "Who Shot Ya (Freestyle)"
**4.** "Good Morning America"
**5.** "Blow Them Horns"
**6.** "Gz and Hustlas"
**7.** "I Feel It (Freestyle)"
**8.** "Interview with DJ Dave Part 1"
**9.** "Imma G"
**10.** "Interview with DJ Dave Part 2"
**11.** "Man of the Hour"
**12.** "Interview with DJ Dave Part 3"
**13.** "Never Die"
**14.** "Hpnotiq"
**15.** "J Dilla (Freestyle)"
**16.** "Interview with DJ Dave Part 4"
**17.** "Get Throwed"
**18.** "Blood Sport (Freestyle)"
**19.** "Prototype"
**20.** "Hard Body"
**21.** "Grammy Family (Freestyle)"
**22.** "A Song for Buffy (Freestyle)"
**23.** "Interview with DJ Dave Part 5"

24. "Dreams"
25. "The Best Rapper Alive"
26. "Imagine"

## No Sleep Til NYC (2007)
Top Dawg

**Released:** December 24, 2007
**Producers:** Clark Kent, DJ Premier, DJ Skee, DJ Warrior, Dr. Dre, Eric B, Havoc, Johnny J, Large Professor, Rakim, Ski Beatz, A Tribe Called Quest
**Featured artists:** Ab-Soul ("Enjoy Life," "The Real Hip Hop (Freestyle)," "Dead Presidents III, "Topdawg Ent."), BO ("Topdawg Ent."), Dave Free ("Can't Be Faded"), DJ Big Mike, DJ Warrior ("DJ Warrior Outro"), Glasses Malone ("Smooth Operator"), Punch ("Kick in the Door," "Halfway Crooks"), Jay Rock ("Smooth Operator")

**Tracks:**
1. "DJ Big Mike Intro"
2. "The Show"
3. "I Ain't No Joke"
4. "Enjoy Life"
5. "The Real Hip Hop"
6. "Dead Presidents III"
7. "It Ain't Hard 2 Tell"
8. "Smooth Operator"
9. "Kick In The Door"
10. "Halfway Crooks"
11. "Cali's Finest"
12. "OG Julio G"
13. "Topdawg Ent."
14. "Death Around the Corner"
15. "Gangsta Party 08"
16. "New Pimpin"
17. "Preach"
18. "DJ Warrior Outro"
19. "Can't Be Faded"

## C4 (2009)
Top Dawg

**Released:** January 30, 2009
**Producers:** Maestro, DJ Infamous, Drew Correa, Bangladesh, Cool & Dre, Swizz Beatz, Robin Thicke, D. Smith, STREETRUNNER, David Banner, The Alchemist, Kanye West, Deezle, Rodnae, Mousa, Sounwave
**Featured artists:** Ab-Soul ("West Coast Wu-Tang," "Take Off Ur Pants," "Still Hustlin'," "Welcome to C4," "Famous Pipe Game"), Punch ("West Coast Wu-Tang," "Phone Home," "Shot Down"), Jay Rock ("Intro (Wayne Co-Sign)," "Still Hustlin'," "Welcome to C4," "Misunderstood"), ScHoolboy Q ("Welcome to C4"), BO ("Welcome to C4"), Lil Wayne ("Intro (Wayne Co-Sign)," "Mr. Carter")

**Tracks:**
1. "Intro (Wayne Co-Sign)"
2. "Best Rapper Under 25"
3. "Mr. Carter"
4. "A Milli"
5. "Bitch I'm in the Club"
6. "West Coast Wu-Tang"
7. "Phone Home"
8. "Compton Chemistry"
9. "Take Off Ur Pants"
10. "Shot Down"
11. "Play With Fire"
12. "Friend of Mine"
13. "Still Hustlin' "
14. "Welcome to C4"
15. "G Code"

**16.** "Famous Pipe Game"
**17.** "Misunderstood"
**18.** "Young & Black"

## *The Kendrick Lamar EP* (2009)
Top Dawg

**Released:** December 31, 2009
**Producers:** Sounwave, King Blue, Q-Tip, Black Milk, Insomnia, The Foreign Exchange, Jake One, Wyldfyer, Pete Rahk
**Featured artists:** Angela McCluskey ("Is It Love"), Ab-Soul ("P&P"), JaVonté ("She Needs Me," "Uncle Bobby & Jason Keaton"), Jay Rock ("I Do This"), BJ the Chicago Kid ("Faith"), Punch ("Faith"), ScHoolboy Q ("Far From Here"), Big Pooh ("Thanksgiving"), Ash Riser ("Determined")

**Tracks:**
**1.** "Is It Love"
**2.** "Celebration"
**3.** "P&P"
**4.** "She Needs Me"
**5.** "I Am (Interlude)"
**6.** "Wanna Be Heard"
**7.** "I Do This"
**8.** "Uncle Bobby & Jason Keaton"
**9.** "Faith"
**10.** "Trip"
**11.** "Vanity Slaves"
**12.** "Far From Here"
**13.** "Thanksgiving"
**14.** "Let Me Be Me"
**15.** "Determined"

## *Overly Dedicated* (2010)
Top Dawg

**Released:** September 14, 2010
**Producers:** Dave Free, Dude Dawg, Kendrick Lamar, Jairus "J-Mo" Mozee, King Blue, Drop Beatz, Sounwave, Tae Beast, Tommy Black, Willie B, Wyldfyer
**Featured artists:** Dash Snow ("The Heart Pt. 2"), Jhené Aiko ("Growing Apart (To Get Closer)"), Ab-Soul ("P&P 1.5"), JaVonté ("Opposites Attract (Tomorrow, w/o Her," "I Do This (Remix)"), ScHoolboy Q ("Michael Jordan"), BJ the Chicago Kid ("R.O.T.C. (Interlude)"), Ash Riser ("Barbed Wire"), Alori Joh ("Heaven & Hell"), Dom Kennedy ("She Needs Me (Remix)"), Murs ("She Needs Me (Remix)"), Thurz ("I Do This (Remix)"), Y-O ("I Do This (Remix)")

**Tracks:**
**1.** "The Heart Pt. 2"
**2.** "Growing Apart (To Get Closer)"
**3.** "Night of the Living Junkies"
**4.** "P&P 1.5"
**5.** "Alien Girl (Today w/Her)"
**6.** "Opposites Attract (Tomorrow, W/O Her"
**7.** "Michael Jordan"
**8.** "Ignorance is Bliss"
**9.** "R.O.T.C. (Interlude)"
**10.** "Barbed Wire"
**11.** "Average Joe"
**12.** "H.O.C"
**13.** "Cut You Off (to Grow Closer)"
**14.** "Heaven & Hell"
**15.** "She Needs Me (Remix)"
**16.** "I Do This (Remix)"

## KENDRICK LAMAR SOUNDTRACK RELEASES

### *Black Panther: The Album* (2018)
Top Dawg/Aftermath/Interscope

**Released:** February 9, 2018
**Producers:** 30 Roc, Aaron Bow, Al Shux, Axel Folie, Baby Keem, BADBADNOTGOOD, Cardo, Cubeatz, DJ Dahi, Doc McKinney, Frank Dukes, Illmind, Kurtis McKenzie, Ludwig Göransson, Matt Schaeffer, Mike WiLL Made-It, Robin Hannibal, Rascal, Scribz Riley, Sounwave, Teddy Walton, Twon Beatz
**Featured artists:** SZA ("All the Stars"), ScHoolboy Q ("X"), 2 Chainz ("X"), Saudi ("X"), Khalid "(The Ways"), Swae Lee ("The Ways"), Vince Staples ("Opps"), Yugen Blakrok ("Opps"), Jorja Smith ("I Am"), SOB X RBE ("Paramedic!"), Ab-Soul ("Bloody Waters"), Anderson .Paak ("Bloody Waters"), James Blake ("Bloody Waters," "King's Dead"), Jay Rock ("King's Dead"), Future ("King's Dead"), Zacari ("Redemption Interlude," "Redemption"), Babes Wodumo ("Redemption"), Mozzy ("Seasons"), Sjava ("Seasons"), Reason ("Seasons"), Travis Scott ("Big Shot"), The Weeknd ("Pray for Me")

**Tracks:**
1. "Black Panther"
2. "All the Stars"
3. "X"
4. "The Ways"
5. "Opps"
6. "I Am"
7. "Paramedic!"
8. "Bloody Waters"
9. "King's Dead"
10. "Redemption Interlude"
11. "Redemption"
12. "Seasons"
13. "Big Shot"
14. "Pray for Me"

# INDEX

**252**